I AM Violet Tara

In Action

Lessons in Mastery

———

Peter Mt. Shasta

Published by Church of the Seven Rays
PO Box 711
Mount Shasta, CA 96067 USA

Copyright 2020 by Peter Mt. Shasta

ISBN: 9798633742657

No part of this book may be reproduced, stored in a retrieval system, or transmitted by any means without the written permission of the author. Request for such permission should be addressed to the publisher at www.I-Am-Teachings.com

Table of Contents

PREFACE 7
FOREWORD 11

CHAPTER 1 15

BASIS OF THE I AM TEACHINGS 15
GOD IS YOUR HIGHER SELF 15
GOD ACTS WHEN YOU SAY, "I AM" 17
THE PATH TO MASTERY STARTS HERE NOW 17
I DON'T BLAME ANYBODY 18

CHAPTER 2 19

BASIC TEACHINGS 19
BECOME THE "I AM" 20
THE DIVINE DIRECTOR 20
RECEIVE WHAT GOD WANTS TO GIVE 22
RIDING THE MERRY-GO-ROUND 22
BECOMING THE OBSERVER 24
BECOMING A MASTER 25
DISCIPLINE TO ATTAIN MASTERY 25
QUESTION AND ANSWERS, CHAPTER 2 27

CHAPTER 3 31

WHAT YOU DWELL ON, YOU BRING TO LIFE. 32
VIOLET TARA MEDITATION #1 33
QUESTIONS AND ANSWERS, CHAPTER 3 38

CHAPTER 4 39

MASTERY IS IN CARING FOR OTHERS 39
SAINT FRANCIS 40
EVERY EXPERIENCE IS AN OPPORTUNITY 42
FOUR THOUGHTS 43
FOUR NOBLE TRUTHS 44
INVOKING VIOLET TARA #2 46
BLESS THE EARTH 46

QUESTIONS AND ANSWERS, CHAPTER 4	50

CHAPTER 5 53

GOD CONSCIOUSNESS AND MASTERY	55
MEDITATION ON THE I AM PRESENCE	56

CHAPTER 6 59

ENERGIZING BREATH	59
MAKE THIS PRACTICE YOUR OWN	61
THREE PRACTICES TO BENEFIT HUMANITY	61
QUESTIONS AND ANSWERS, CHAPTER 6	66

CHAPTER 7 67

STORY OF BUDDHA'S TOOTH	69
QUESTIONS AND ANSWERS, CHAPTER 7	71

CHAPTER 8 73

RESOLUTIONS	74
SPONTANEOUS APPEARANCE OF VIOLET TARA	76
GLOBAL SANGHA OF VIOLET TARA	77
MEDITATION ON THE PERFECTION OF GOD	78
QUESTIONS AND ANSWERS, CHAPTER 8	80

CHAPTER 9 83

GOD BLESS THAT	83
IMPORTANCE OF SELF-WORTH	85

CHAPTER 10...89

VIOLET TARA MEDITATION: CONCISE FORM	89

CHAPTER 11...93

I AM AFFIRMATIONS	93

CHAPTER 12...99

EXTRA MEDITATIONS AND PRACTICES	99

MEDITATION FOR GUIDANCE 103
INNER HEALING USING MINDFULNESS 104

CHAPTER 13..113

EXPERIENCES WITH VIOLET TARA 113

Other Books by Peter Mt. Shasta

"I AM" the Open Door. Fourteen discourses given by ten different Ascended Masters who appeared to Peter Mt. Shasta in their light bodies to teach how to contact your inner God Self and bring its Mastery into daily life.

"I AM" Affirmations and the Secret of their Effective Use. How to make affirmations work through the practice of meditation. Contains many affirmations for use in different areas of life from spirituality to relationship and business.

"I AM" the Living Christ: Teachings of Jesus, Profound teachings of the New Testament edited in light of the Gnostic texts. Jesus's own use of I Am affirmations, as well as his acknowledgment of the Mother aspect of God, are highlighted.

Lady Master Pearl, My Teacher. Biography of Pearl Dorris, assistant to Godfrey Ray King and Director of the Saint Germain Foundation of San Francisco. Saint Germain sent many of his students to her for training on how to contact the I Am and apply it as a Master in daily life.

Search for the Guru: Adventures of a Western Mystic, Book I. First part of the autobiography of Peter Mt. Shasta describing his spiritual awakening, journeys to India, adventures with Ram Dass, Maharajji, as well as many other saints and sages.

Apprentice to the Masters: Adventures of a Western Mystic, Book II. Second part of the autobiography of Peter Mt. Shasta, describing his meetings with the Ascended Masters Saint Germain, Kuthumi and El Morya, and the training on the application of the I Am Teachings in daily life. Unlike any other book.

Step by Step: Ascended Master Discourses. Talks by various Ascended Masters given to a group led by Pearl Dorris in the 1940s. The power released through these talks is amazing.

My Search in Tibet for the Secret Wish-Fulfilling Jewel. Adventures of Peter Mt. Shasta in Tibet, where he was sent by both the Sixteenth Karmapa, the Dalai Lama, and Saint Germain.

I AM the Violet Tara, Goddess of Forgiveness and Freedom. Further teachings in Mastery incorporating the ancient practices of Tibetan Tantra, leading to Self-Mastery. This is the introduction of Violet Tara, which precede this book. It shows how to invoke Her as a force for good in your life—and for the benefit of humanity.

It Is What It Is. Further adventures of Peter Mt. Shasta on his path of Self-Mastery. Exciting, often humorous stories about his experiences living in Mount Shasta.

Preface

Violet Tara came into being in the winter of 2019 when the Ascended Master Saint Germain appeared with the request that I bring forth teachings about Her. In a sense, this was Her rebirth because She was known to a group of women initiates in China in the 11th century as Goddess of the Violet Mist.[1] However, under the patriarchy of the Chinese aristocracy, knowledge of Her was suppressed. When those women, who practiced the secret Taoist teachings of energy conservation, ascended into oneness with the Rainbow Body, knowledge of the Goddess of the Violet Mist faded into obscurity.

However, those ancient teachings on the use of breath, energy, consciousness, and focus, to transcend the normal bounds of human existence, were also developed and preserved in India and Tibet in the teachings of Tantra (Sanskrit: *Vajrayana).* Saint Germain now wishes to introduce these teachings to the outer world, free of ancient cultural associations and religious dogma. The tantric teachings of the White, Green and Red Tara have already been taught by many of the Tibetan lamas who have migrated throughout the world, giving instruction as best they can. They have been limited, however, by the constraints imposed by their various lineages, such as the injunction to only give the teachings in Tibetan, and only to those who have taken refuge in the

---

[1] *Immortal Sisters: Secret Teachings of Taoist Women,* translated and edited by Thomas Cleary (North Atlantic Books, Berkeley, CA).

Buddha Dharma, completed preliminaries (*ngondro*) consisting of a hundred thousand prostrations, as well as four other practices, with advanced instruction going only to those on three-year retreat. Even then, that is only a beginning.

Many Tibetan teachers, from the Dalai Lama to Trungpa Rinpoche, have said, as Tenzin Wangyal Rinpoche says here, that the long-hidden teachings should now be presented in the West. It is Saint Germain's wish also that these ancient teachings come forth.

Some Tibetan masters might find it strange that I teach these practices to Westerners who have not done certain preliminary practices or who do not have certain understandings. The teachings were traditionally maintained as secret teachings...as a protection against dilution (and) through the misunderstanding of unprepared practitioners. (The practices) were never taught publicly nor given lightly...but conditions in the world have changed, and so I am trying something different. I hope that by teaching (them), the tradition will be better preserved, and more people will be able to benefit from it.[2]

---

[2] Tenzin Wangyal, *The Tibetan Yogas of Dream and Sleep,* p. 18 (Shambhala, Kindle Edition).

In an attempt to foster Self-Mastery, I gave the basic teachings in *I AM the Violet Tara, Goddess of Forgiveness and Freedom.* The book immediately became a best-seller, which demonstrated how hungry people are for this knowledge of how to bring forth into the outer world the inner, sacred feminine consciousness.

Introductory knowledge of the inner God Self was transmitted by Saint Germain through Guy Ballard (pen name: Godfre Ray King) in the 1930s and became known as the I Am Teachings. These were also timeless Vedic and Taoist teachings presented for the first time in English rather than the traditional Sanskrit.

It has been my work, under the guidance of the Masters, to continue the gradual unfoldment of these teachings in a modern format so that all can easily understand and apply them in daily life. So, after publishing the first book on Violet Tara, I tried to ascertain how best to make these tantric teachings available more widely.

In response to the requests of hundreds of readers, I gave a series of ten online webinars and also formed a Violet Tara private Facebook group to further elucidate the practices. This book is a condensation of what came forth through those online teachings and the experiences shared by participants.

Being part of the Violet Tara Sangha (community), that emerged as a result of these efforts, has been most heartening. Even though the sangha has been online, it has served as a vehicle for the basic truths: that our consciousness binds us all together, and that the fundamental quality of enlightened mind is loving compassion *(Bodhicitta).*

I would like to thank all those who have helped birth Violet Tara. This book is especially the result of the work of Thomas and Christine Carlisle, CeeCee Clark, Juno Dawson, Kalee Gracse, Anita Kress, and Zorra Victorya. Many thanks also to those who shared their Violet Tara experiences with the Violet Tara Facebook Group online. Some of their stories are presented here.

Much of the text in this book is drawn from the ten online **Violet Tara Webinars** the author gave from the end of 2019 to the beginning of 2020. To fully receive the energy transmitted during the live talks, I AM affirmations, and guided meditations, download the audio mp3 files from the author's website. All his other books and various videos are available there for download:

www.I-Am-Teachings.com

Foreword

It is a true privilege to offer our foreword to *I AM Violet Tara in Action*. We feel blessed to know Peter Mt. Shasta as spiritual teacher and friend. Peter has lived an extraordinary life, as recounted in his autobiographical books, *Adventures of a Western Mystic: Books I and II*.

In these volumes, as well as in his other writings, Peter's integrity, humility and spiritual adeptship are revealed as he pursues the path of Self-Mastery and oneness with his I Am Presence under the guidance of the Master Saint Germain.

In his previous book, *I Am the Violet Tara, Goddess of Forgiveness and Freedom*, Peter introduced the tantric practice of the Violet Tara, given to him by Saint Germain, who originally brought forth the teaching of the Violet Transmuting Flame in the 1930s. This new book, *Violet Tara in Action*, was given birth through a series of Violet Tara meditations conducted by Peter Mt. Shasta in ten webinars with students from around the world from October 2019, to January, 2020.

In these online meetings Peter gave advanced Buddhist and Vedic teaching in a way that can be understood and incorporated into the busy lifestyles of modern seekers, providing a means to enter into higher states of consciousness to bring about effective change in our lives and the planet.

Violet Tara is indeed the Goddess of Forgiveness and Freedom. She embodies the action of the Violet Flame and we call Her forth to assist us at this time of great change on the earth.

She dissolves negative energy, transmutes the karmic consequences of past actions, extends to us Her unconditional forgiveness, liberates us from the delusion of duality, and raises us into a higher frequency.

The Violet Tara practice also helps you realize the divinity within yourself. With this practice, you re-create yourself as Violet Tara—an aspect of your I Am Presence—and become filled with Her deep compassion and profound love.

Peter explains simply and concisely how to do this practice. One could spend many years at the feet of a qualified teacher to receive the inner essence of these teachings, but Peter is making them readily accessible for the western aspirant. How fortunate we are to have someone born and raised in the West with this knowledge and experience!

To participate in these meditations with Peter is to become acquainted with a soul filled with loving kindness and patience toward anyone seeking this knowledge. He demonstrates the divine love and Mastery the Ascended Masters have taught. He helps us harness the full power of God, as is our birthright, to assist the Earth.

In joining with people of like mind all over this blessed Earth, we walk together bearing mercy and forgiveness. Knowing that a community of like-minded people is doing this practice around the world, establishes a perpetual ongoing *sangha,* a community of brothers and sisters that reinforces our individual and collective spiritual work.

The individual and creative ways we are invited to do this work is limited only by our imaginations. Peter, like Padmasambhava, has stated that there is no one way to do the Violet Tara meditation, that you have to make it your own. Using the template he has given, we can do this work with whatever spiritual practice we are already using. It is our hope that all students of Saint Germain will incorporate the Violet Tara meditations into their own existing practice and make it their own unique offering.

It is our prayer that we collectively establish our unity with each other as well as with our God Self. We may find that it is those we unconditionally love and forgive, who restore our own souls.

Thomas and Christine Carlisle
March 15, 2020

Chapter 1

Basis of the I Am Teachings

The Tantric teachings in this book are not something that I invented, but are ancient teachings as old as humanity, taught by different people at various times.

The aim of tantric teachings is to help you understand how your mind works and to become its Master. As a Master, you can then help others. This requires the development of forgiveness and compassion, which is the domain of the feminine energy of Violet Tara.

The purpose of this book is to further the teachings and meditations that engender forgiveness and compassion through the generation of Violet Tara—who is an emanation of your God Self. She is also a manifestation of the feminine aspect of the Violet Consuming Flame—an activity taught by Saint Germain with the approval of the Maha Chohan.

The core of the teachings Saint Germain gave to Godfre Ray King in the 1930s was:

God is your Higher Self

Many of us grew up with a picture of God as the old man with a white beard that Michelangelo painted on the ceiling of the Vatican's Sistine Chapel. That's how many of us grew up thinking of God. In India and Tibet people grew up with all kinds of Gods and Goddesses. However, people also understand these

Gods are aspects of their own consciousness. The True Self is your *Atman,* what occultists call the Monad, Tibetans refer to as the *Dharmakaya*, and I refer to as the I Am Presence.[3]

No matter how you relate to God, the Divine essence is within you as surely as every ray of the sun contains the essence of the sun and every drop of the ocean has the essence of the entire ocean.

This I Am Presence exists above you in a more etheric realm, yet anchors itself as an etheric focus called the unfed flame (Sanskrit: *Jyoti*) just to the right of the sternum. Ancient pictures have portrayed this as a shining light in the center of the chest, as in the following image of Mother Mary showing the Immaculate Heart. It is immaculate because it is the focus of God, untouched by thought or ego. It is this consciousness that you can access in meditation.

Immaculate Heart of Mary

---

[3] *My Search in Tibet for the Secret Wish-Fulfilling Jewel*, by Peter Mt. Shasta, p.86.

Bring your awareness to that place where your Higher Self is anchored. Contact God there. That is the Divine microphone through which God hears your every thought and feeling. Don't think God is far away, for your heart could not beat or your lungs breathe without God.

The next step in the teachings given by Saint Germain is that:

God Acts When You Say, "I Am"

This is an ancient teaching well known in India. In Sanskrit *Aham Brahmasmi* means "I Am Brahman (God)." The use of I Am affirmations is based on the Vedic science of vibration which take the form of mantra recitation. Whatever words are associated with the God vibration come into being. Hence, when you transcend the ego in meditation and say "I Am," you call your Higher Self into action.

The next step is to realize that you do not achieve Self-Mastery somewhere else.

The Path to Mastery Starts Here Now

We are unlimited God Beings who came into the physical Earth realm to experience something, to learn something that could only be experienced in duality. Hence, you can only have enlightenment if you first experience ignorance.[4] You can only

---

[4] Buddhists say that *samsara* (delusion) and *nirvana* (enlightenment) are opposite sides of the same coin.

understand goodness if you first experience evil. You can only understand obedience by first acting in disobedience. God does not want slaves, but people who understand what is going on and take responsibility for themselves.

Hence, we need to realize that we are where we are in life as a result of our own actions, choices we made either in this or past lives. Realizing this, cures us of victimhood—feeling someone else is responsible for our situation. Here is where the path starts, with the realization that you are here at this point in space and time because you chose to be.

I Don't Blame Anybody

This knowledge allows us to work on ourselves and not look for someone else to be the source of, or solution to our problems. We don't need someone else to do something before we can progress. The path starts at your own feet. Where you are standing right now is where your path begins.

Chapter 2

Basic Teachings

Meditation

Sit still with your spine straight, either on the floor cross-legged or seated in a chair with legs uncrossed and feet flat on the floor. You may either close your eyes or keep them partially open, gazing downward. Place the tip of your tongue against the roof of your mouth to complete the subtle energy circuit. Turn your attention inward and observe the rise and fall of your chest, the inbreath and outbreath. There is no strain, just keep observing the breath, which acts like a mantra to keep your attention focused. Should thoughts arise, label them "thinking," and return to the observation of the inbreaths and outbreaths.

Gradually, your mind will slow and you will see there is a quiet, non-conceptual space in the thinking process. At that moment, you may realize that there is a thinker and something else, something observing the thoughts.

What is that?

In Sanskrit the saying is *Tat Twam Asi:* **You are that!**

Meditate on that!

Become the "I Am"

Close your eyes, still your mind and turn your attention to the center of your chest where the God Presence is anchored. Say silently to yourself, "I...I...I" and feel what happens. It's taking you inward and upward into your God Self. Meditate on this "I". Meditation on this "I" anchors you in the God consciousness of the Father and Divine Will.

Now, open your eyes and say, "Am." From your heart, say, "Am." This is the God consciousness of the Mother that releases the action of the "I" into the world with Divine Love.

This simple meditation calls into the world the power of "I" consciousness released into the world through the "Am" consciousness.

"I" combined with "Am" is will and power combined with love. The two principles working together through the field of experience lead to wisdom. This is the activity of God the Father with God the Mother to produce the Divine Child, which is Wisdom.

Whatever words you say after "I Am," you bring forth into the world. Thus, be careful what you say and what you think, for that is what you create.

The Divine Director

Every morning when I wake up, the first thing I do is look up at my I Am Presence. I don't usually see it, but I know it's there. I say:

I Am the Great Divine Director of my day.

The Divine Director is like the CEO of a corporation, and it's your corporation, your life. There's a Master known as the "Great Divine Director" and his job is to wake you up to the Great Divine Director of yourself.

Call on your Great Divine Director right now. Imagine a sun in the center of your chest and just feel:

I Am the Great Divine Director of my life, my being, and my world.

As you continue to feel "I Am the Presence of the Great Divine Director of my life, my being, and my world" it radiates out, not only affecting your life, but affecting the lives of everyone around you. Whatever city you are in, you are invoking the Great Divine Director for everyone. You are invoking it for the entire planet.

Sometimes, I say:

I Am the Great Divine Director of all the governments of the earth.

Can you imagine that? Can you feel the Power of it?

I Am the Great Divine Director of my business.

I Am the Great Divine Director of all my relationships.

For further affirmations invoking the Great Divine Director, see my book, *"I AM" Affirmations and the Secret of Their Effective Use,* which gives affirmations for every aspect of your life.

Receive What God Wants to Give

When I first found these teachings, I experimented by decreeing for all sorts of things. "I want this." "I want that." When I got them, though, I realized they were not really helpful. They were not truly of benefit. So, I said, "Dear God, please show me what You want me to have." You can ask to be shown what it is you want to create.

I Am being shown what to create.
I Am being shown the next step.

So now when you say, "I Am", you'll only create what is in the flow from God. You no longer create out of ego. Don't get me wrong, the ego is not a bad thing; it's actually a valuable tool that helps us function in the world. Just don't take your direction from it.

Your job is to become familiar with your ego and train it the same way you would train a puppy. A puppy wants to go this way and that way. But after a while, you train it to walk by your side. You train the ego to do the same. You teach your ego to be obedient to your I Am Presence. To walk quietly by your side, not pulling and tugging you in every direction.

Riding the Merry-Go-Round

There's an image I would like to share with you to help you understand your own ego and how it works. Picture yourself in an amusement park, riding on a merry-go-round. When you gaze away from the merry-go-round, you see all kinds of other attractions.

You see other rides that you can go on. You see people riding in bumper cars laughing as they crash into each other. You see a big Ferris wheel that goes way up high, and a shooting gallery where you could try to win a prize. Then you notice people enjoying food from the many food vendors who sell ice cream, hot dogs, cotton candy, and other treats.

This is a great symbol of our world. We go through life like we're riding a merry-go-round, seeing all the attractions of the world. Some we want, others we don't. The Buddhists refer to this as the Eight Worldly Dharmas. There are four things we are attracted to: pleasure, fame, praise, and gain; and four things we want to avoid: loss, pain, blame, and a bad reputation.

Another thing that happens when we ride the merry-go-round is that we're told "try to reach the brass ring." If you catch one of these rings, you get a free ride. But trying to catch the brass ring also increases the risk that you will fall off and hurt yourself. Consider this another metaphor for life. We're always striving and reaching and grasping for something "out there."

Instead of looking at all the other attractions or reaching for the brass ring, there's another option. When riding the merry-go-round, you can look at the center of the merry-go-round. In the center, you'll see a mirrored pillar that anchors and stabilizes the merry-go-round. And, because it's mirrored, when you look at the center of the merry-go-round, you see yourself.

So, by looking to the center, you take your attention away from all the distractions that are whirling around outside the merry-go-round and you see yourself. You're no longer thinking about grabbing the brass ring, you're looking at yourself.

That's what you do in meditation, take your attention off the attractions and aversions, the pleasures and pains, all the concerns of the ego, and just feel the stillness and the Oneness that transcends your personality. Then you will realize you are already enlightened. That enlightenment is your true nature. You are one with Jesus, with Mary, with Saint Germain, with Violet Tara. You are one with all the Masters. You are one with God.

Becoming the Observer

If you keep practicing meditation, after a while you will become aware that the self you are identifying with is not your real Self. It's the self that has been programmed.

As a child growing up, in order to preserve yourself, you realize you have to develop an ego. I remember doing this consciously when I was very young. I felt completely vulnerable, so I watched what other kids did. I watched certain personality traits and I thought, "hmm, that worked for that kid, maybe it would work for me." So, I sort of synthesized an ego to learn to deal with the world.

You may have had to pretend to be tough because other children tried to push you around. Maybe you were told you need to be pretty or handsome or dressed a certain way. And you got praise or gifts when you fit that mold. So, we learn all these ego traits to survive in the world. We play a role and we figure out what works and what doesn't.

The only problem is, after a while, we begin to identify with that role and those traits, and we start to think that's our real self. The purpose of meditation is to help you transcend this invented role that we call ego. It's still there as a tool to help us function in the world, but we have to learn that the ego is not who we really are.

Becoming a Master

There is a place in meditation where you experience no self, where you're completely immersed in the Oneness, but you can't function in the world from there. You have these great saints, like Ramakrishna, who would go into this state of Oneness, and needed to be taken care of because they could not care for themselves. You may reach this state of Oneness for a few moments and find pure bliss, but you can't drive a car in that state or go to work to earn your living there.

The process of becoming a Master is learning to be in tune with the Oneness while being aware of your ego and staying in harmony with the world. This ability to be an observer of the self is essential to Mastery. It's a form of "non-meditation" (called *maha ati* in Sanskrit or *Dzogchen* in Tibetan), which is meditation in the midst of daily life.

Discipline to Attain Mastery

When I asked Saint Germain, "What should I charge for the book, *I Am the Violet Tara?*" I heard, "Twelve dollars and thirty-four cents." I thought. "That's a strange price. Why should I charge that?"

When I wrote it down, I saw $12.34, and understood the lesson that when you go to school, you start with the first lesson, then go to the second, then the third and fourth, and so on. The same is true in becoming a master. You start at the beginning with some basic meditation, then go to the next step and the next, and so become gradually more skilled. This is what Mastery is about. You don't jump around. You don't just take a webinar and become a master. It takes time, dedication, and doing one thing at a time in the correct order.

The Tibetans would not even talk to you about the teachings in this book unless you had finished the preliminary practices called *Ngondro*. The first preliminary practice is to do 100,000 prostrations. If you do nothing else everyday but these prostrations, you might finish them in 3 to 6 months. There are four more practices which also require you to do 100,000 repetitions of each.

It's a lengthy process and the Tibetan Llamas will not teach the things I have put in this book until the student has completed them all. They are hesitant to give these teachings to Westerners because they know our tendency is to try one thing and, if it doesn't work right away, to go do something else. We tend to get distracted with things like watching TV, going to the café, being with friends, or getting a text from someone, etc. Our Western lifestyle tends to keep our minds constantly spinning.

If you want to make progress you have to sit down and work on your Mastery. You don't need to do 100,000 things before you get started. You can work on your Mastery today by learning the lessons and doing the meditations presented in this book. Take one step at a time and enjoy the journey.

Question and Answers, Chapter 2

Q: Is it good to use the I Am Presence for health and wealth, or only for fulfilling the will of God? Is it selfish to use the I Am Presence for health and wealth?

P: No, it is not selfish to use the I Am Presence for health and wealth. God doesn't want you to starve or to suffer. God likes us all to be healthy and abundant; although, sometimes, there are certain lessons we are here to learn. And remember that God doesn't always go in a straight line. I once drank out of the Ganges because I thought that was what God wanted me to do. It took me a several years to recover from that experience; however, what I learned because of it ultimately put me in touch with my I Am Presence. Not a straight or very pleasant way to get there, but well worth it.

When I grew up on the East Coast, I knew very wealthy people who owned multinational corporations and not one of them was happy. They were all worried about the price of their stock or if there was going to be a strike or government regulation. When you want wealth, the important thing is to say, "Dear God show me the right way to become abundant."

Abundance is not necessarily a dollar amount. Wealth does not lead to happiness. The kind of wealth that leads to happiness is the kind where you are able to prosper other people, so I affirm:

***I Am the abundance of God made manifest
in my hands and use for the benefit
of humanity.***

Although I've always had enough for what I need in the moment, there have been times when I didn't have very much, which was always perfect for the lesson that I needed at the time.

Q: If one is focused on the I Am Presence, is it still necessary for one to visualize what he or she wants, such as a particular job or wish? In other words, if one concentrates on their I Am Presence only and does not visualize or consciously try to manifest, is this okay?

P: If you are meditating on the I Am Presence, at some point you'll get guidance. Guidance might come to you in the form of an image. By developing a close rapport with your I Am Presence, guidance may come to your heart at every moment. After meditating on the I Am Presence, if you are walking down the street, you might get guidance to go the other way, or to do this, or that. The I Am Presence will give you guidance automatically. It might be also helpful to say:

***I Am come forth in and through me
throughout this day. Bring about the
Divine plan in all activities.***

When I started to get the feeling to do webinars, I said:

I Am being shown how to do this.

I tried out several software applications and was guided to a particular one. The point is that once you get the guidance to start an activity, it's good to call on your I Am Presence and call It into action.

I suggest you pick a time every day when you meditate on your I Am Presence and feel your closeness to it. Practice this as often as you can. Some people develop the habit of talking to their Presence. My teacher Pearl could have a conversation with her I Am Presence. She could ask it a question and get an answer.[5] When you develop this type of relationship with your Presence, you won't need to go online and type something in a search box because you have all the answers you need by chatting with your I Am Presence.

---

[5] To learn more about Pearl read, *Lady Master Pearl, My Teacher* (Church of the Seven Rays, 2014)

Chapter 3

It is through forgiveness that we achieve freedom and Mastery. Holding onto anger or resentment about another person or situation binds us to that person or situation while creating negative karma that we later need to release. That's why it is important to look at any issues where we hold onto old wounds.

As the Goddess of Forgiveness, Violet Tara can help you deal with these issues. The word "forgive" is the word "for" or "before" and "give." What forgiveness means is to give someone the opportunity—for your own personal growth—to do whatever it is they did that hurt you. This doesn't mean you want or invite people to injure you. It means that you acknowledge that you are where you are meant to be at this point in space and time, not by accident, but as a consequence of your own previous choices and actions—either in this or past lives.

You made an agreement to come to Earth at this time to be in relationship with people who agreed to play in your drama. Different people will show up at different times in your life, sometimes as a friend, a lover, an enemy, maybe just as someone who pushes your buttons. An old saying is, "If you think you're enlightened, get into a relationship." When you're with someone you love and are drawn to be with, for sure your buttons are going to get pushed.

It's up to each of us to look at difficult situations and ask ourselves, "What is this showing me about myself"? When I experience a negative reaction to someone, I know this person is showing me something about myself. It is said that when you point your finger at somebody, there are three fingers pointing back at you. This is absolutely true. That's why, when you experience a negative reaction to someone, instead of trying to change the other person, look at what in you corresponds to what that other person is doing.

I think most of us experience negative reactions to people or situations daily. When that happens, it's important to say, "I take responsibility for this situation". I'm here voluntarily, and so is this other person. I may not be able to change them, but I can change my reaction. That is where the freedom is. That is why Violet Tara is also the Goddess of Freedom. As long as you are having these reactions to other people, you can't be free because you're bound by those emotional reactions.

What You Dwell On, You Bring to Life.

We are confronted daily with the choice of where to put our attention. It is this power of attention that creates our lives, our feelings, what we relate to, and how it affects us. I once had friends who thought red was evil, so when they saw me driving a red car, they stepped back in horror, thinking it was something evil. They couldn't even see it was their friend driving. They created red to be evil and they lived their life accordingly.

What your attention is on, you create. That's why it is extremely important what you decide to put your attention on. If your attention is continually on all the political conspiracies, you live in a world determined by what news story you read or what the news commentator says. Since we have to put our attention on something, better to have it on your I Am Presence, a God or Goddess. It's up to us what we want to invoke in our lives.

When you invoke Violet Tara, you are transmuting your karma, you are transmuting any toxins in your body, you are raising yourself to a higher frequency. Any negative ideas you have about yourself get burnt up by Violet Tara's violet flame.

Violet Tara Meditation #1

Close your eyes and turn your attention to the center of your chest where your God Self is anchored. Be still and observe the rise and fall, the inbreath and the outbreath. There is no strain, just keep observing the breath, which acts like a mantra to keep your attention focused. Let go of the past. Let go of the future. Don't try to figure out anything. Just be completely in your body in the present moment. Feel in the center of your chest a sort of warmth or think of it as the feeling of love, a gold pink glow. If a thought comes up you just label it thinking and let go of it. Just come back to observing this energy in the center of your chest. It's sort of a soft spot. It's a place we may try to avoid because there is heartache there sometimes, but we don't have to put a label on it. Just feel God's love for you there. This is where your God flame is anchored. You could not take a breath without that flame, so you are connected to God at every single second. You don't have to try hard to reach God. God is aware of your every thought, feeling, emotion, and in fact is causing you to breathe.

You could not take your next breath without God, so just be grateful to that as you stay in that awareness.

Request from Saint Germain the Violet Tara empowerment:

Beloved Master Saint Germain, please empower Violet Tara in my life right now, fully self-sustained, a living Goddess for the benefit of all. Oh, great Violet Tara, Beloved Divine Mother, You, who are an emanation of the Light from the Heart of Creation with which I Am One, I implore you. Release your Violet Fire of purification through my mind, feelings, and world. Purify and transmute wherever purification is needed this very moment. Thank You! I know it is already done

As we have been invoking her, a shaft of Violet Light has come down. See this Goddess appearing in the atmosphere, emerging from a ball of violet light with pink and gold in the center. She becomes more and more visible and takes on the form of a beautiful Mother Goddess in luminous violet robes in front of you. She nods and smiles to each of us with tremendous love and compassion. Just feel her love pouring out to you as beautiful rays of violet light streaming from her heart to your heart. She holds out her hands to you and rays of violet light stream from the palms of her hands into you, into your hands. Gradually she comes closer…and you say to her:

Beloved Tara I ask you to become one with me.

As our bodies increase in frequency and we become filled with more and more light, we too begin to shimmer with Violet Light. She now becomes so bright that we can hardly see her form. She is now a ball of Violet Light like an amethyst with a sun in the center. Suddenly, she dissolves and those rays of light go into our own hearts. She enters our hearts. Her essence and your essence merge.

Now affirm and feel:

I Am Violet Tara.

Feel what it is like to be her. Feel great beams of Violet Light radiating outward from your heart, from the center of your forehead, and from the palms of your hands. Feel this transcendental sense of forgiveness.

I forgive everyone and I know I am forgiven.
I am forgiveness filling the Earth.

Say and feel

I Am Tara of Violet Fire.
I Am the Purity God Desires.

You may also say the traditional mantra of all the Taras (In Tibetan Buddhism there are 21 Taras, all with their own qualities and functions):

Om Tare Tuttare Ture Swaha.

(Meaning: Great Victorious Mother, embodiment of all enlightened activity, I ask for liberation for all beings. So be it!)

Say and feel:

I Am the Presence of God manifesting as Violet Tara, radiating out to humanity.

The Violet Light from your heart expands to enfold the Earth in this mantle of Violet Light and you see everyone on Earth whose heart is now filled with Violet Light feel gratitude and forgiveness and love for each other. You are not only burning up your karma, you are helping heal yourself and everyone on Earth. Continue to amplify this blessing:

***I Am Violet Tara, radiant Goddess from the heart of creation. I Am pouring forth Love, Purity, Wisdom, and Forgiveness wherever needed, transmuting everything into its inherent perfection and bringing God's Divine plan to Earth this very moment.
So Be It!***

We can also say:

I Am Violet Tara now pouring forth forgiveness and God's blessings into the minds, hearts, worlds, and governments of the Earth, of all world leaders, of all people everywhere.

Keep feeling yourself as Violet Tara, imagining your body as an amethyst with this light pouring out through it and continue to say and feel:

I am Violet Tara. I am the purity God desires.

In whatever location you are, it fills with Violet Light, uplifting, raising, transmuting, and forgiving all. Send it wherever you want.

Now, let go of this visualization and return to what is called Basic Emptiness. This is the consciousness of meditation where there is really no self, no attachment to anything, where you're not in the ego, just pure consciousness; awareness without limit. Gradually, dissolve yourself as the Violet Tara and return to yourself as an energy being. Continue absorption in non-conceptual awareness. Feel gratitude for what you have just experienced as you return to your own Buddha nature or Christ Self, free of ego clinging and negative emotions, which have now been purified. We are graced to do this work together, blessed by the Ascended Council of Light, by Saint Germain, the Violet Tara, and above all by our own God Presence. We now further invoke Beloved Violet Tara:

Violet Tara sit above me in a pink lotus blossom, radiating Violet fire wherever I go throughout the coming week so even if I forget about you, please bless everyone I meet. Wherever I go, please radiate the Violet Consuming Flame to bring love, forgiveness, and perfection into every situation.

During the week, you will notice that suddenly people feel that blessing, and the situation will be magically transformed. They will feel that light because it is an aspect of God, your I Am Presence. We close our practice with words of gratitude:

Thank you, Violet Tara, for being with me and coming forth in your splendor. Please be with me always and come into action wherever needed. I am grateful.

Questions and Answers, Chapter 3

Q: How long should we keep Violet Tara in our hearts before letting Her go?

P: That is up to you. If you had 15 minutes, you could hold Her in your heart for 15 minutes. Sometimes you don't have much time. Let's say you only have a minute or even 10 seconds. Hold Her for as long as you have time, knowing that the longer you hold Her, the deeper the effect will be. The sincerity of your intent is what is important.

Q: Are we not full of light ourselves and therefore also have the violet light within us all the time? Is it just that we give it attention every now and then?

P: It's there all the time to some degree. Just like violet light is in the room as part of the clear light, but we don't see it. You have all the colors within you. So, yes, violet light is within you all the time. The purpose of this practice is to call it forth.

Chapter 4

The I Am Teachings focus on spirituality in action. There are various other paths that bring you to God consciousness, especially in India, where you cease to exist as an individual and you merge with the consciousness of Oneness. Although this merging leads to bliss, it does not lead to Mastery in the world. You cannot drive a car while immersed in Oneness, nor work, nor raise children.

We actually came out of that Oneness to incarnate on Earth and experience duality. We can still return to that timeless, formless consciousness to refresh ourselves, but our spiritual growth is in taking part in the world and the affairs of society. Mastery is in being aware of the Oneness while at the same time functioning in the world as a creative, loving, compassionate being. Violet Tara practice generates the love and compassion we need to achieve the freedom necessary to be a true Master.

Mastery is in Caring for Others

It's possible to become so focused on achieving Oneness that you forget about others and never develop compassion. Many ask, "How do I know I'm making progress on the spiritual path?" My friend, Ram Dass said:

If you start feeling superior because of your spiritual evolution, you are headed in the wrong direction. But, if you are feeling more

love and compassion for others, that's a sign you're making progress.

People frequently ask, "I don't feel the love that I wish I had. Where is the love?" Many people believe that if they got into a relationship, they would feel more love. But love has to be found first in you and does not originate from the relationship. It is a big turning point when you realize that the love you feel comes from within yourself, not from others.

If you do a good deed and your picture appears in the newspaper and you get letters of love and admiration, does that make you feel love? Do you feel love in your heart? You have to have love in your heart first, before you can love someone else. You feel love for another because that person reflects the love that is within you. When you find that love, you never feel devoid of love again.

That's the beauty of this practice. When you meditate on "I Am Love," you're sending the Divine Love within you flowing forth to others. You are the source of love. It's a simple practice that can be done wherever you are. The more you practice the "I Am Love" meditation, the more love you'll feel, for the love you are sending out into the world comes back to you amplified ten-fold.

Saint Francis

Francis of Assisi, back in the 12th century, discovered that happiness is in helping others. The movie about him that I highly recommend is *Brother Sun, Sister Moon.* He was a playboy, good looking, rich, and had a lot of friends. Everyone loved him.

However, his life was soon to change. He went off to war thinking it was going to be a great and glorious thing, but he was captured, almost died in prison, and when he came home, he had what is now called Post Traumatic Stress. He no longer cared about ordinary life.

One day, Jesus appeared to him and said, "Rebuild my church." He thought Jesus meant the run-down church on the edge of town, but Jesus was actually referring to the *sangha*—the community of believers known as the Church.

His work soon attracted a lot of followers, including some of his old friends, who likewise now realized the futility of superficial life—what in India is called *samsara*—the pursuit of endless distractions and pleasures that turn out in the end to not satisfy. They now found that real happiness came from helping others and so formed a community of monks and lived together outside the city. This part of the prayer, attributed to Saint Francis, beautifully reveals his transformed view:

O Master, let me not seek as much
to be consoled as to console,
to be understood as to understand,
to be loved as to love,
for it is in giving that one receives,
it is in self-forgetting that one finds oneself,
it is in pardoning that one is pardoned, it is
in dying that one is raised to eternal life.

"Dying" here refers to death of the ego—the little self that wants attention. This poem contains the essence of the path to Mastery. Our questions should be:

How can I help others?

The Violet Tara practice is one way to provide that help. It is an avenue to Mastery because you are invoking the Goddess whose sole purpose is to give love, forgiveness, and freedom. As you merge with Her, you pour Her love out to others and so develop that same love and compassion within yourself.

Every Experience is an Opportunity

Some on the spiritual path focus on personal gain, how to use spiritual energy to acquire what they want, if not things, then how to achieve bliss and personal freedom. That is more the path of Hinayana Buddhism, which focuses on personal liberation. The Mahayana and Vajrayana paths are about seeking to become enlightened for the benefit of others—to become a Master to alleviate suffering.

However, as you become enlightened, you realize others are a part of yourself anyway, even enemies and those who stress you out. They are all part of yourself and are in your life for a reason. You agreed before you were born to be in association with these people. They are here to teach you something. Once you realize they are a part of you and are here to offer you some gift—that by overcoming the challenge they provide, you gain something—then you no longer feel anger or frustration but see them as an ally.

Try to embrace every experience as an opportunity. If you get stopped by a policeman for speeding, you can bless the officer. When I was driving across the country, I was stopped by a police officer. Instead of going into fear when I was pulled over, I said to myself "This is an opportunity for my own Mastery." So, instead of being angry or upset, I told the policeman:

> *You have a good heart.*
> *I know you are helping many people.*

He stopped in his tracks and his jaw dropped open. I don't think anyone he ever stopped had said that to him. I gave him a copy of my book and he was reading it by the side of the road as I drove off. If you embrace every experience as an opportunity, you will receive a great blessing.

To gain perspective on the spiritual path, contemplate the Four Thoughts That Turn the Mind to the Dharma, and the Four Noble Truths, which reveal universal teachings taught by the Buddha:

Four Thoughts

Contemplate the Four Thoughts That Turn the Mind to the Dharma, which reveal universal truths taught by the Buddha:

The Preciousness of life: Human birth is a precious gift that we have been given. It's not to be taken lightly. It's important to recognize this and be grateful for every minute of life, for every incredible opportunity.

Impermanence: Nothing lasts forever. Everything dies, even universes. Your life could end at any moment.

Karma: Every action has a consequence. We are where we are in our lives as a result of our previous actions. When you realize that, you dissolve your sense of victimhood. You don't blame others for your circumstances but take responsibility for your life.

Samsara: Wandering endlessly in pursuit of things that are not permanent. Instead, pursue what is permanent, what survives human life. That shift in focus is what Saint Francis experienced. The pleasures of the moment did not give lasting happiness. This realization leads many to the spiritual path.

Also, contemplate the following teachings of the Buddha:

Four Noble Truths

Do not expect lasting happiness on earth: Happiness and suffering come and go, often unexpectedly, as the circumstances of life are like ever-shifting sands. Permanent happiness only comes from what is eternal.

Suffering is caused by desires or aversions: If you are attached to a certain pleasure and don't get it, you will be unhappy. Or, if you seek to avoid something that is unavoidable, suffering is inevitable.

Lasting happiness only comes when you neither seek nor avoid anything, but rest in inner equanimity.

There is a way to avoid suffering: You don't need to drift through life buffeted by the vagaries of external experiences and events. There is a path to lasting happiness.

The Eight-fold path: This is an outline of the spiritual path to happiness. It offers methods of self-development leading to wisdom, compassion, enlightenment, and freedom. These eight practices are prerequisites for Mastery:

1) **Right Understanding**: understanding the nature of reality.
2) **Right thoughts**: having thoughts of selfless service, love, and compassion.
3) **Right speech:** speaking only words that are true and avoiding gossip, hurtful words, and excessive talking.
4**) Right action:** doing only what promotes benefit for all.
5) **Right effort:** being diligent on the path of Mastery.
6) **Right livelihood:** having an honorable profession that benefits others.
7) **Self-observation:** observing one's thoughts.
8) **Meditation:** cessation of thought leading to limitless awareness.

Invoking Violet Tara #2

The following practice of invoking Violet Tara can also be used to invoke other Gods and Goddesses. It is a basic invocation where you see the Deity in front of you, which becomes more and more real, and then dissolves into light. That light goes into you and you realize, "I Am That."

Many spiritual paths encourage the worship of various Gods, Deities, and Ascended Masters, whether Jesus, Mary, Lakshmi, Mahakala, Ganesh or whomever it might be. The goal is to realize God within and realize the Deity or Master is also as an aspect of yourself.

The Violet Tara practice helps you to get in touch with that inner aspect. It's not just imagination; it is the creative aspect of God, or creative aspect of your Self.

Bless the Earth

Invocation of Violet Tara:

Beloved Goddess Tara, Mother of the Violet Flame of Forgiveness, help us overcome the illusions of the world. Free us from ignorance and help us to achieve enlightenment. Grant us the ability to forgive and feel compassion for others. Clear all negative energy and raise our consciousness. We pray to you: Come to us now Violet Tara, Mother of the Violet Fire.

Violet Tara materializes in front of you. This Goddess made of Violet Fire emanates exquisite violet light from Her heart and the palms of Her hands.

She has the same violet energy as Saint Germain, blazing out from Her. You don't need to get it from him for you can now generate it yourself. Violet Tara is a spontaneously self-arising Deity. You can ask Her to manifest in front of you. She arises out of your own consciousness—an aspect of and manifestation of your own I Am Presence. If you have trouble visualizing, just feel Her.

Feel the love and compassion of this Goddess of Violet Fire as She looks at you with infinite tenderness. Her love pours out to you and She cleanses all your wounds and removes all sorrows from your heart. She's helping you feel the love that is within you.

As you do this, Her energy purifies the room you are in—purifying your home, neighborhood, the city in which you live, and the entire Earth. Other Violet Taras around the world are joining together and enfolding the Earth in a beautiful Violet Light.

Violet Tara in front of you dissolves into a ball of violet light. As you watch, this beautiful light merges with your heart. Say and feel:

I Am Violet Tara.
I Am Tara of Violet Fire.

Feel that light go into every cell. Your body is no longer physical. You realize that every atom is empty space. The particles are simply energy, thought, and vibration. As this consciousness of the Violet Fire penetrates every atom of your body, it accelerates the frequency of the atoms, and your body becomes this wonderful amethyst light. Say and feel three times:

I Am Tara of Violet Fire,
I Am the Purity God Desires.

If there is pain in any part of your body, see that part of your body as an amethyst that starts to glow with inner light, and then hold that focus.

Now that you have become Violet Tara, use your Divine Power to benefit humanity. Gradually ascend off the Earth and look down. The Earth is a large ball beneath you with various dark clouds where there is war, suffering, and confusion. You can help alleviate those conditions by sending rays of violet light into those places and situations.

Please join me above (location of your choosing) and feel the love in your heart for those who live there. Send a beam of violet light from each hand, dissolving the dark clouds, and say:

I Am Tara of the Violet Fire dissolving and consuming all negative energy, thought forms, and suffering, beneath, in, around, and above **(location you have chosen).**

Watch the dark clouds dissolve. Send beams of violet light into the buildings and people. See the streets filled with violet light. Now blaze those rays of violet light beneath the city, down into the Earth, then blazing back up, sending great rays of that purifying light shooting into space.

Go to the capital of your own country, or any location you choose, wherever it is needed, and blaze forth the Violet Flame. Say and feel:

I Am Tara of Violet Fire,
I Am the Purity God desires in this city,
these people, and their government.

Now, gradually dissolve the visualization of yourself as Violet Tara and return to basic emptiness. This means you are no longer Violet Tara, but you are not your personal mind or ego either. Achieve this state by observing the inbreath and outbreath, the rise and fall of your chest. If a thought comes up, just dismiss it with the label: "thought."

Let your consciousness expand outward. Realize you are an unlimited being, you are eternal, you are without beginning or end. You have always been and will always be. Let go of holding onto any kind of definitive concept. You extend throughout the universe...beyond the universe, for you are the Creator. Now, come back to the awareness of your form. Observe where you are, who you are, and your name—but know you are not that. You are aware there is an ego, but it does not define you. It is just a vehicle to help you function in this world of illusion. You are beyond name and form, beyond thought and feeling. You are unlimited.

You can end by asking Violet Tara to stay with you throughout the coming week. Imagine there is a pink lotus blossom above your head, big enough for Her to sit in. She sits cross legged in the lotus blossom and you say to Her:

Beloved Tara, I thank you. Please reside
above me and help me during the coming

week. Please dissolve any negative thoughts or feelings I might have. You have my permission to bless everyone I come in contact with, whether I remember you or not. Please come forth and bless everyone I encounter with the Violet Fire of Forgiveness.

Then let Her go with this prayer of gratitude:

I give thanks, O Tara, for your grace, guidance, and blessings. Please help me to remember you. Be with me always. I thank you.

Questions and Answers, Chapter 4

Q: Since there seem to be so many political problems currently, it appears we are in some sort of transition as humankind together. Is this true?

P: Absolutely. We are in a transition time. As far as politics go, you have to trust that everybody is where they are meant to be to bring about God's Divine Plan. Sometimes that comes about through what we would call a disaster or confrontation.

There is a great story about this in the *Ramayana*. The Gods needed a bad guy, someone to be the villain, so they could teach humanity good and evil, right and wrong, and lessons like that. Nobody wanted to be the bad guy. Finally, Ravana volunteered. He was the equal of any of the Gods but volunteered to play the bad guy so that humanity could witness this drama of the battle of good and evil. This battle brought out the good and evil in the people involved.

We are going through a similar confrontation now, where all the negativity and all the good are coming to the surface. Rather than blaming, hating, or saying someone is evil, send blessings to them. I visualize the angels of the Violet Fire and Violet Tara over the nation's Capitol and the White House every day. This lets you do something about it rather than adding more negative energy. It's not just the United States government. All the governments of the world are going through upheaval, with riots and protests happening in all the capitals.

Rather than feel fear and trepidation, see this time as an opportunity to grow. By sending Violet Tara to these troubled areas, you can grow rather than get depressed. This is a wakeup call for us to move into action, to forgive, gain our Mastery, and freedom. My mother used to say, "It's better to light a single candle than curse the darkness." You may think, "What good is it to light one candle?" But if a million people each light a candle, the light becomes very bright.

Chapter 5

Invoking Violet Tara gives our own I Am Presence a form to come through. When I first came to Mount Shasta and began to receive the I Am teachings from Pearl, she recommended I read *Unveiled Mysteries*.[6] The book portrayed the I Am Presence as a beautiful being with a rainbow aura. It was so dramatic I thought it was a metaphor, and artist's interpretation of the Higher Self. I could not imagine it was an actual being.

I used to wake up at night and see various Ascended Masters standing by my bed talking to me. I recognized Kuthumi, El Morya, and Saint Germain. They were communicating on a higher level and I could not hear them, but they allowed me to see them so I would know they were working with me.

Several nights in a row, I became aware of a new Master. I wondered who he was and wanted to hear what he was saying, so before I went to bed, I said, "I am being shown who this is, and his name."

In the middle of the night I awoke to see a ball of light near the ceiling surrounded by beautiful rainbow colors. I sat up in bed and demanded, "Who are you"?

Very clearly, I heard, "I Am you...I Am your own God Presence."

I was so shocked, I passed out and didn't awaken until morning. That was my realization that the I Am Presence was a real.

The I Am Presence rarely contacts our human personality directly, rather it contacts us through an

---

[6] *Unveiled Mysteries* by Godfre Ray King (Saint Germain Foundation, 1939).

intermediary etheric body known as the higher mental body, soul, or *sambhogakaya*.

Meditation helps strengthen our connection with the higher mental body so we can better receive guidance. Just like lifting weights helps build muscles, the more you meditate, the stronger the connection with your higher mental body becomes. Just like any relationship, the more you interact the more familiar you become. This familiarity allows you to receive a clearer communication from your I Am Presence.

Ever wonder how you are able to feel so connected to someone on the phone, even if they are far away? Or, you're in a group like our Violet Tara Facebook Group and you feel close to everyone participating even though you've never met them in person. That's because when you are connected with someone, even over the phone or online, your higher mental body is there with them. Wherever your attention is, your higher mental body is there also.

In the I Am teachings this is called projected consciousness. You can project your consciousness, not only anywhere on Earth, but anywhere in Creation. You can do this because your higher mental body can travel outside time and space with the speed of thought. It can communicate with anyone else's higher mental body or participate in any activity at any point in Creation. It's one of the reasons meditation makes us feel more connected with others and keeps us from feeling cut off from people or from events happening far away.

At the time of the illusion known as "death," the higher mental body lives on. It then merges with the I

Am Presence, the Rainbow Body, completing the ascension process.

God Consciousness and Mastery

Many spiritual teachings dwell only on God consciousness, beyond all sense of form or self. These Advaita teachings promote deep meditation to completely dissolve identification with ego. You go into a state of bliss and oneness with all that is. The only problem is that there is no one there to experience it, as the self has merged into an ocean of pure consciousness. Ramakrishna, the great Indian mystic, compared this dissolution to tossing a grain of salt into the ocean. The salt merges with the ocean and there is no longer any individuality.

You become one with your God Self. Even though that consciousness is beautiful, you cannot function in the world while in that state. There are pictures of Ramakrishna in that cosmic consciousness where he had to be fed and taken care of. He had no awareness of himself—only bliss, but that is not Mastery in the world.

Then there is a state of consciousness where you have access to the Oneness but are still aware of yourself as a separate being in the world of duality. This is the awareness of the Ascended Masters. They are God Beings aware of themselves as active agents for change in the human world. They are what is called *Mahasiddhas*, Sanskrit for those who have attained all the powers of self-realization. They function in whatever realm they wish.

Mastery is learning to bring the awareness of the higher worlds into human consciousness and action in daily life. This is a purpose of Violet Tara practice, to learn to bring your own God Presence into action in the world as a specific Deity.

The reason you can influence the world is because we are all connected like drops in the ocean of pure consciousness. What one drop experiences is experienced by all the other drops, because we are all part of the same ocean. Scientists have found that sub-atomic particles are still in communication with other sub-atomic particles that were part of the same atom, even if separated by a distance of light-years. What you do to one particle affects the other particles. The same is true for us. What one does, affects all.

Violet Tara is an expression of your I Am Presence, whom you invoke to be effective in the world. She is an expression of your own Divinity. Invoke Her to create love, peace, harmony, healing, forgiveness, and freedom, for yourself and others.

Meditation on the I Am Presence

Be still and observe the rise and fall of your chest, the inbreath and the outbreath. Say and feel:

I Am the Presence of God right here now.

See the focus of your I Am Presence as a golden light glowing in the center of your chest, surrounded by the beautiful pink glow of Divine Love. Rays of pink light tinged with gold go out into the hearts of all humanity as you say:

I Am Love radiating to humanity.

Say and feel:

I forgive everyone,
everyone that has ever hurt me.
I call for forgiveness between all the peoples
of the world, between all nations, races, and
religions. May everyone be forgiven and feel
forgiveness in their heart.

As your light goes out to humanity and starts to turn violet, say:

I Am Tara of Violet Fire,
I Am the purity God desires.

As the Violet Light envelops the Earth, say and feel:

I Am Wholly Pure and Perfect. I call on Violet Tara to reside above me in a beautiful lotus blossom. During the coming week, I ask Her to come forth wherever needed and bless everyone I contact and think about. I Am the Great Divine Director of my life, bringing about perfection wherever I Am. I Am grateful to Saint Germain for making these teachings available to humanity. I thank you and it is done.

Chapter 6

Energizing Breath

I'd like to give you an energizing breathing practice. If you feel a little depressed or are lacking in energy, you can do it to lift your spirits. It uses the yogic Bellows and Holding Breaths and is especially good right before meditation.

When I first started meditating, my breathing slowed so much I thought maybe I was not getting enough oxygen and I would take a few deep breaths. Well, if you do this practice before meditation, your body and your cells will be so oxygenated and energized you will have no concerns.

As you do this breathing exercise, you're pulling energy up through the subtle channel which goes up the center of your spine and energizes your chakras. It increases the heat in your body and will help you get going in the morning or anytime you really want some extra oomph. You will also be enabled to better feel the violet light in every cell.

Do not overexert yourself. (Consult your doctor if you have any health issues or questions as to any possible detriment from breathing exercises). Sit with your spine straight. Exhale all the stale air in your lungs. Then, with mouth shut, breathe rapidly in and out through your nostrils 40 times. Then inhale deeply and hold your breath for about 40 seconds. Then, exhale fully.

If you wish to intensify the energy, repeat this entire process of Bellows and Holding Breath three times. After the last exhalation, sit still and feel the energy circulating through your body. Keep the tip of your tongue against the roof of your mouth, completing the energy circuit. Feel the energy going down into your feet. The soles of your feet have chakras, which feels like a sun under each foot. The light you have generated is going back up through your legs, into your solar plexus, on up the central channel in your spine, up to your heart. Feel the warm sun in your heart and the light radiating to every cell in your body. Light also pours out your 3rd Eye (*Ajna* chakra) and also up through the top of the head to the thousand-petalled lotus (*Sahasrara* chakra).

The subtle nervous system in your body is being filled with rays of light emanating out into space. It's going through your shoulders, your arms, into the palms of your hands. Your fingers are energized with light. Above you is your I Am Presence, a sun of golden light surrounded by rainbow colors, which is all the goodness and wisdom you have accumulated through your many lifetimes, radiating into space. Say inwardly, think, and feel:

I Am the Presence of God
That I Am.

Sit in this awareness for a few minutes and feel:

I Am the Presence of the Living God.

If your mind wanders, just observe the inbreath and outbreath. Any thought that comes up, just label it "thinking" and come back to the breath. Allow your awareness to settle in the heart chakra *(Anahata),* which is slightly to the right of your sternum (not the physical heart).

Make This Practice Your Own

We're about to begin a meditation, but before we do, you should know that Violet Tara does not have to be visualized as a Goddess. You can simply imagine violet light or amethyst light instead. It's not the visualization that makes this practice work. It works because of your inner attunement, your inner connection with your I Am Presence, which is anchored within your heart chakra. It's the combination of your thought, spoken word, and your love that makes it all happen.

Everyone is going to do this work in their own way. As Padmasambhava said:

Mingle this practice with your own being.

It always amazes me when I give a meditation practice and I think everyone is doing the same thing. Then, later, I hear that people were doing something slightly different. They've made the meditation their own, which is fine as long as it leads to the same awareness.

Three Practices to Benefit Humanity

There are many ways to use the Violet Tara meditation to benefit humanity. Three methods I will give here are to visualize yourself: 1) above the earth, sending light rays downward, 2) on the earth, radiating outward to humanity, and 3) within the center of the earth, illuminating the entire planet.

Meditation in the Center of the Earth

Some practitioners transport themselves to the center of the earth in their Higher Mental Body through projected consciousness, using the affirmation, "I Am in the center of the Earth." Others may visualize traveling there on a subterranean vehicle from inside Mount Shasta, or others may use a UFO that goes up to the North Pole and then down inside the earth. Any of these methods work.

Transport yourself by whatever means you choose to the center of the earth. Here there is another world that some call Shambhala, vibrating at a higher frequency with its own inner sun. It's incredibly beautiful here. You are in a beautiful field. In front of you is a round temple with marble columns.

Outside this temple are the Lords of the Ten Directions. They will protect and send you energy while you are inside. In the sky are a ring of angels and above and beyond them are the Archangels. Beyond them are the Seraphim, Thrones, Powers, and Dominions. These are majestic beings who have gathered for you while you invoke Violet Tara.

You enter the temple. Seated around the walls are the seven Masters, who are the Chohans (heads) of the seven rays. You bow to each other in acknowledgement of the inner God Presence. You sit before them in the chairs provided, then still your mind by observing the rise and fall of your chest, the inbreath and outbreath. You are not thinking about the past or the future, not trying to understand anything or make anything happen. You are at this moment in this focal point of light.

Request from Saint Germain the Violet Tara empowerment:

Beloved Master Saint Germain, please empower Violet Tara in my life right now, fully self-sustained as a living Goddess for the benefit of all beings.

Then request further empowerment from Violet Tara herself:

Oh, great Violet Tara, Beloved Divine Mother, You, who are an emanation of the Light from the Heart of Creation with which I Am One, I implore you. Release your Violet Fire of purification through my mind, feelings, and world. Purify and transmute wherever needed this very moment. Thank You! I know it is already done.

See Violet Tara appearing in the atmosphere. First, you see just a violet light. The Goddess emerges from that ball of light. She becomes more and more real, an exquisite woman clothed in a violet robe.

The living, breathing Goddess is in front of you. She is the embodiment of compassion and has tremendous love for you. She is your enlightened sister, helping you to forgive everyone. She also forgives you for every unkind thing you may have ever done. She now asks you to forgive everyone else. Feel Her love. Say and feel:

I Am forgiveness.

Now She dissolves back into a ball of violet light and enters your heart. You merge, and Her essence and your essence become one. Her consciousness is your consciousness. Feel the Violet Light in your heart radiating out into space. Say and feel:

I Am Violet Tara.

Rays of Violet Light shoot from your heart, fill the entire Earth, and radiate out into space. Everyone on Earth is affected by this Violet Light.

Say Her mantra three times, feeling the violet light streaming out through you, healing, and burning up planetary karma. This light affects everyone because we are all linked in consciousness and residents of the mind of God:

I Am Tara of Violet Fire,
I Am the Purity God Desires.

You may also say Her Sanskrit mantra 108 times:

Om Tare Tuttare Ture Swaha

Deepen this blessing to humanity by saying and feeling:

I Am Violet Tara, radiant Goddess from the heart of creation. I Am pouring forth Love, Purity, Wisdom, and Forgiveness wherever needed, transmuting everything into its inherent perfection and bringing God's Divine plan to Earth this very moment. So Be It!

After this transmission, return to basic emptiness, free of thought, without desires or aversions, just pure awareness.

In closing, say to Tara:

Beloved Violet Tara, please sit above my head in a pink lotus blossom, radiating

Violet Fire wherever I go throughout the coming week. Even if I forget about You, bless everyone I meet. Radiate the Fire of Forgiveness, the Violet Consuming Flame, to bless and heal everyone and every situation.

You are not the same being you were an hour ago. Feel the Divine Goddess energy pouring through you. Saint Germain is grateful to you for doing this practice, for you are now an emissary of the Violet Flame, an assistant to him in his work. Instead of calling on him all the time to send the violet fire here or there, you are yourself now a transmitter of the Violet Flame of Forgiveness.

Gradually open your eyes and become aware of your surroundings, still observing the inbreath and outbreath. You are completely in the present moment, feeling:

I Am the Presence of the living Goddess in action throughout this day.

You don't need to act serious but keep your awareness on the center of your being and observe what thoughts go through your mind.

Don't identify with the thoughts that come and go, for they are only shadows while you are the sun. You now know how to call forth love, compassion, and forgiveness at any time.

Questions and Answers, Chapter 6

Q: I don't always have time to do the whole Violet Tara practice. Can I just visualize Violet Tara and ask Her to transmute whatever we're working on?

P: Yes, of course. You can ask Violet Tara or Saint Germain to go into action at any time in any situation. You don't have to sit down and do a whole long invocation. It's just for your benefit and upliftment, it's good to do a formal practice on occasion. The more power you generate as the practice becomes habitual with you, the better you get at invoking Violet Tara and Her violet flame without doing a lengthy practice.

Q: Is the tunnel on the side of Mount Shasta real? Can we go there? Is it available to only very highly evolved people?

P: On the Harmonic Convergence, which I believe happened in 1987, I was meditating when a being appeared in front of me and took me out of my body to the side of Mount Shasta to this tunnel. We traveled on a subway-like train that was suspended and propelled by magnetism. In about 20 minutes we reached the center of the Earth. Don't bother searching for the entrance for it's not something you're going to find in the physical plane unless you significantly raise your vibratory frequency.

Chapter 7

Tantric practice is based on the understanding that there is a sea of awareness that encompasses everything and you are a creator that is one with that sea. Since your mind is everywhere, it's up to you to create what you want and to interpret that experience. Life puts you in touch with yourself as a Creator. As such, there are all kinds of practices you can do to invoke what you wish. When you say, "I Am" you bring forth what follows those words through the creative power of your Light. So, what do you want to be?

You can say and feel:

I Am a White Fire Being from the heart of the Great Central Sun.

Or:

I Am the Great Divine Director of my life and world.

Or:

I am Violet Tara, Goddess of Forgiveness and Freedom.

Your words, thoughts, and feelings determine what you are. Hence, you need to observe your thoughts at every moment to control your being and the effect you are having on others.

You can be whatever you want. You are limited only by your own mind. There are many statements you can make and practices you can perform to make your life as you wish. Generally, it is best to remain with one practice until you have mastered it.

Saint Germain gave the Western world the basic teachings of the "I Am" in the 1930's through Godfre Ray King. He taught about the Ascended Masters and the power of the words, "I Am." He didn't teach meditation as a part of it until the 1970's, through Pearl Dorris, my teacher. Now he has asked me to bring forth advanced teachings on the nature of mind that make the teachings more powerful and open the door to liberation from the world of illusion.

Someone asked me, "Is this inclusion of Eastern methods your own embellishment or does it come from Saint Germain?" My answer is that this is definitely at the request of Saint Germain. During my time studying the "I Am" with Pearl, former assistant to Godfre Ray King, I completely immersed myself in those teachings. However, after Pearl's ascension, I was guided to go back and once again immerse myself in Tibetan Buddhism.

I had begun to study under the Bodhi tree in Bodhgaya, India, and continued to study there with Burmese monks. On my return to the States, I ran into Trungpa Rinpoche and received initiations from him. Later, I received instruction from Chagdud Rinpoche and the 16th Karmapa, who sent me to Tibet, to assimilate certain aspects that could only be transmitted in certain locations that had been empowered by Padmasambhava.

When I talk about Buddhism, it's not the religion but the mind practices to which I am referring. "Buddha" means someone who is awake. Thus, Buddhism is the science of awakening—not only your mind, but your heart and speech, so you can function in full awareness and enlightened activity—which is the work of Mastery.

Violet Tara practice is only one doorway through which I am introducing these practices—one way to awaken to the magical nature of your own mind. This is the science of enlightenment and Mastery that can be applied to and enhance your daily life.

Story of Buddha's Tooth

I'd like to tell you this story because it reveals something of the nature of tantra. There was a merchant who was going on a long journey. His elderly mother asked if he could bring Her something from a distant town. She had heard a rumor that they had Buddha's tooth and she wanted him to bring it back for Her. She had been told that if you had one of these teeth, you would become enlightened very quickly. She was elderly and did not want to die without attaining the Rainbow Body. She knew that owning this tooth of the Buddha would facilitate Her ascension.

The merchant told his mother that he would bring the tooth and left town. Then, he got busy on his journey and when he came back into town, he realized he had forgotten the tooth. On his way to his mother's house, empty-handed, he found a dead dog by the side of the road and took one of the teeth, wrapped it in a beautiful silk cloth, and tied it with a ribbon. "Mother, I brought you Buddha's tooth, as you asked," he proclaimed proudly.

His mother was so excited that she worshipped the tooth with fervor. She did prostrations to the tooth, invoking and merging with the consciousness of the Buddha. She soon became fully enlightened and ascended into the Rainbow Body. The moral of the story is that what we focus on we bring into being. It didn't matter that it was a dog's tooth and not Buddha's tooth, for to the merchant's mother it was the focus she needed to attain self-realization.

Every day you are faced with the decision on what you want to place your attention. When you get up in the morning, you can focus on all the negative things in your life and end up with them cycling around in your head all day, or you can focus on the light within, tune in to yourself as a creator, and create perfection. Clean your mind. Clean out all the dregs of those negative associations and focus on what is positive.

This is the perfect path to Mastery. Many times during the day, negative thoughts or feelings come up that you can change. If someone cuts you off in traffic, you might get angry and want to swear at them. But you can see it differently. Look for ways to be compassionate. Maybe they were rushing to the hospital because their child was in an accident. Or maybe they simply made a mistake. There may have been times when you did the same.

Try to see whatever happens that causes anger or pain as something that can help you grow in your Mastery. Call on Violet Tara to help you forgive others for the flaws we all share. The intent of these practices is to help you turn your mind around and instead focus on the positive. By visualizing Violet Tara, you get in touch with Violet Tara within yourself. You have the power to forgive and that sets you free.

I met with somebody the other day who began telling me their problems. Instead of focusing on their unfortunate situation, I visualized this woman as Violet Tara, and kept holding that visualization. She suddenly stopped talking. It was like a lightbulb turned on. She lit up. We both just sat there, speechless, in this beautiful light. Now, if I had felt sorry for her, I would have got sucked into her despair and depression, leaving us both feeling bad. Instead, when I said, "I Am Violet Tara in action in you, and the Violet Tara in me is blessing the Violet Tara in you," we ended up blessing each other.

Questions and Answers, Chapter 7

Q: I know we are all one but how do I convert it into an experience?

P: That requires meditation. You can experience oneness in meditation when you realize that the Presence in you is also the Presence in me. Then you treat people as an aspect of yourself. Jesus said:

I say to not only love your friends but love your enemies.

Friends and enemies are a part of you and they are in your life for a reason. So, thank the people who challenge you, for they give you the lessons you need. Forgiving them is your freedom.

Q: Do you do this practice every day, and do you do it at a fixed time?

P: I try to do it in the morning when I wake up, but I'm very busy these days so I do it whenever I can. However, first thing in the morning is the best time to do a couple of quick affirmations. One of my favorites is:

I Am the Great Divine Director of this day.

Also, before you go to sleep, look up to your I Am Presence, even though you may not see It. Know that It is there and say and feel:

I love you God, thank you for this day. May I go forth tonight to learn and serve. May I wake up in the morning a better person, remembering what I have learned.

These are two simple things to do every day. Each one takes maybe 15 seconds. Everybody can do these.

Chapter 8

The Internet exemplifies how we are all connected through God. We have the illusion that we're alone but we're all connected. It may seem we are connected to only a few friends but the reality is that when we are online, we are connected to more than 3 billion others. God is the same—a consciousness that permeates all creation, with each of us as a terminal. We're all like individual websites with unique appearances, characteristics, glitches, beauty, and purpose.

Regardless of our individual differences, we're all connected to each other through God's Universal Consciousness. You realize, in the enlightened state, that you are everywhere, in everybody, and there is no limitation. Enlightenment is being unlimited.

Mastery is beyond enlightenment, for you are not only unlimited but are still able to function as an individual. This is why it's so important to regard other people as aspects of yourself—because everyone is. We are all parts of the same God Consciousness, the same God Presence. Even if someone gives you a hard time, try to acknowledge God in that person, that they may have been placed there to challenge you and help you overcome some weakness.

Meditation helps you attain this realization. You see who you are from outside yourself and realize your personality is only a program on your computer screen. If you don't like parts of the program, re-write them!

First, observe how the program works. As you meditate on the program, one part of your mind observes the functioning of another part. It is like activating an anti-virus program. You get the option to delete the virus. Go ahead and press DELETE.

When you become impatient or angry, realize it's just a glitch in your ego program. You don't have to identify with these signals. You see it as just part of the lesson you're learning. You can accept this person who irritates you as a manifestation of God, like yourself. You don't really know what their purpose is but, if their behavior triggers something in you, then it is something to look at in the program. Rewrite the program to serve you better and take a step toward Self-Mastery.

Resolutions

Toward the end of every year, people ask, "Have you made a New Year's resolution?" I think there's something profound in that. Maybe we can all look at ourselves and ask, "Is there something I would like to leave behind?" We don't even have to wait until the end of the year, we can do it now.

Observe something you would like to leave behind. You could say, "I see I have had a habitual reaction to that person, condition, or idea, and I'm going to be free of that this coming year. Take a minute and view your past like a movie. Pick an incident where you got triggered into a negative response. Then, like a character in a play, see how you can play your role differently. Instead of speaking sharply to someone, be more loving. See how to change your role. The same situation is going to come up again and again, giving you the opportunity to play your role differently until you achieve Mastery in that situation. Turn your attention inward and say:

*I am now dissolving and consuming that
in the Violet Consuming Flame.
It is gone! Thank God!
From now I replace it with God Perfection.
I now identify with my Master Self,
my I Am Presence, Who is wholly pure
and perfect.*

You can tell you're making progress as your negative responses become less frequent. You begin to have more compassion, patience, and understanding for people. Then you are making progress.

If you think you're not progressing fast enough, or that these practices are too difficult, or you don't have time to practice, just do something good for someone. You don't have to sit in meditation for long hours or do countless prostrations. Just look around and see what you can do for someone.

It doesn't have to be complicated. It could simply be a smile, opening the door for someone, or saying a kind word. Maybe there's someone you often see who makes you think, "What a nasty person, I wouldn't want to be around them."

What would happen if you went up to that person and said, "Hello, how are you today?" or "Nice day, isn't it!" Even if they respond negatively, you've done something for someone else and you will feel good about it. Eventually you will see results, even if it's slow as an icicle melting. There was a waitress in a café I frequented who seemed nice to everyone else but was always grumpy toward me. For over a year I smiled and tried to joke with her but she always gave me the same grim expression. I kept saying:

I am Divine Love enfolding her. I am the Violet Consuming Flame dissolving and consuming any negativity in her.

Then, one day she burst out laughing at one of my silly jokes and from then on, she smiled when I came in, and was pleasant from then on.

It doesn't have to be someone you see negatively. It might just be the teller at the bank or the checker at the store. You can say, "Have a beautiful day," or "You're doing a great job here," or "You're very kind." It's easy. The more you do it, the more you'll enjoy doing it. Pretty soon, people will even begin to like you.

Many people are so lonely. However, you can change that just by speaking to them. Something like 45% of people over 50 don't have a single person they can talk to. I saw a posting on Craig's List from a grandmother asking to spend one day of the Christmas holiday with a family. She was alone and just wanted to be part of a family for one day and offered to help cook dinner. When you see someone who looks miserable or cranky, sometimes they are feeling lonely or are in pain. Many of us take their negativity personally, but it rarely has anything to do with us.

Spontaneous Appearance of Violet Tara.

I would like to share with you something that happened recently. In the middle of meditation, Violet Tara appeared spontaneously. This was the first time

I had seen Her face to face without invoking or visualizing Her.

When you begin this tantric practice, it takes some effort at first to imagine Her as real. But like anything else, the more energy you put into it, the more real She becomes. After previously invoking and visualizing Her many times, Violet Tara chose this moment to appear. Suddenly, there She was, smiling, as She placed Her hand on my head in blessings. Violet Tara then thanked me for starting this group and for all the work we're doing to invoke Her into action.

A few days before this, I did a prostration full out on the floor, imagining Her in front of me. I touched Her feet with my hands and said, "Beloved Violet Tara, I love You. Please be a real presence in my life to help other people." Several days later, this was Her response.

Sometimes things don't happen exactly when you want them to, or think they should, but they happen in their own perfect Divine time and order. This was the Divine time for Her spontaneous appearance.

Global Sangha of Violet Tara

I love that the book Saint Germain asked me to write, *I AM the Violet Tara,* inspired a Facebook group where all who are doing these practices can communicate. Community, known as Sangha, is one of the Three Jewels of Buddhism. The other two jewels are Buddha (consciousness) and Dharma (spiritual practice). Whether you join this group or practice on your own, I am aware of the love, forgiveness, and compassion you generate going out to benefit humanity. Our vow to attain enlightenment for the benefit of others, and in so doing become Masters, uplifts the mass consciousness. I also feel a personal blessing from the Violet Tara Facebook Group and wish to thank those who are the organizers. I invite you to join with others around the world as we daily initiate a wave of Violet Fire that sweeps the Earth. Visit: www.facebook.com/groups/VioletTara/

Meditation on the Perfection of God

Be still and observe the rise and fall of your chest, the inbreath and the outbreath. Say and feel:

I Am being shown what I would like to leave behind in the coming year. I call on Violet Tara to surround me with a pillar of Violet Light. That Violet Fire is blazing up, in, around, and through me and through my aura, dissolving and consuming anything less than perfection by the power of God, which I Am.

I Am Violet Tara sending the Violet Consuming Flame throughout the Earth, dissolving and consuming everything less than perfection. I Am divine wisdom, forgiveness, and love flowing forth to humanity. I Am being shown how I would like to be different, what qualities I would like to develop in myself. I now see myself as that new person. I Am being shown new ways of acting toward others and toward life itself. I will no longer see myself as a victim. I take full ownership of my thoughts, feelings and emotions. I go forth as a Master Presence, to serve and aid others in whatever way I can. I call on the Ascended Masters to come forth and help me.

You may not hear the guidance audibly. You may simply wake up in the morning with a knowing. You may feel an impetus to do something different, or simply to complete projects you are working on. It doesn't mean there is going to be a dramatic change, but frequently big changes in our life do come unexpectedly. It's not that everything changes at once; you may be shown a plan that will unfold over time. As things come up in your life, you will have a knowingness that it is right. You will feel in your heart that this knowingness is the Divine Plan. This is how meditation in action will manifest in your life. Invoke your I AM Presence with the affirmation:

In the morning when I awaken, I Am remembering what I have been shown and I Am manifesting God's Divine Plan in my life.

When you awaken you may say and feel:

I now joyfully accept the God Presence that I Am, and I rejoice in the Divine Plan my God Presence has for me. I Am the God Presence in action, now and always.

Questions and Answers, Chapter 8

Q: How do I get guidance?

P: Let go of everything. Just rest in non-thinking, non-being. You may be aware of your in-breath and out-breath, the rise and fall of your chest. If thoughts arise, label them "thoughts," and go back to your breath, the rise and fall of your chest...in-breath and out-breath...rise and fall. Gradually, your mind slows down. You begin to dwell in the space between thoughts—the emptiness—empty of thoughts and emotions, but full of awareness and peace. You are no longer identified with an ego, but aware of a larger Self that is one with all, filled with trust and knowing.

That Self, which you can feel in the area of your heart, knows what to do, knows the answers to everything, and knows the Divine Plan for your life. However, it may not tell you what to do, for that might keep you from being spontaneous, from acting in the moment—which is where growth and Mastery are learned.

You may hear all sorts of voices telling you what to do, and grasp at them as the guidance you sought. Ignore them. Rest in the silence and affirm with love and certainty:

I Am being shown what to do in perfect Divine Order, and I am doing it perfectly.

Continue to dwell in the silence, feeling the energy of your True Self filling your awareness. That knowingness fills even the cells of your body, keeping them functioning according to Divine Plan. Trust that every breath you draw comes from the Presence that you are, and that every beat of your heart is a gift from that same Loving Presence. That Presence that gives you life will guide you perfectly. As you remain calm in that Presence, you will know what to do when the moment arrives—and you will do it. As you rise from meditation, go forward and affirm:

I am going where I am meant to go, doing what I am meant to do in perfect Divine Order.

Tune-in to your heart, to the omniscient Presence within. This is the indwelling Presence that knows all and that will guide you to your destination. The guidance appears as a feeling. Trust in that feeling.

As you go forward, you will feel either more energy and confidence or less; if more energy, that is confirmation you are following the Divine Plan; if less, you are following the ego-mind or the suggestions of others. Stay with the feeling in your heart. That feeling is the guidance you seek.

Chapter 9

God Bless That....

Many people are upset about the world situation. That upset takes your attention away from your basic goodness. It also makes it harder to do your spiritual work. Daily we're faced with news stories, which may be true or not. Although these events and stories can be disturbing, there's one simple thing we can do to disengage, and that is to bless them—whatever they are. Just say:

God bless that situation.
God bless that person.

A friend of mine in high school used to say that, no matter what he did, his mother would say, "Why bless your soul." Even when he hit a baseball through the window, she would say, "Why bless your soul." He remarked how that made him feel good instead of sad. It meant that even if he did something bad, he was not bad. He was still okay.

When you try to assign blame, there's really no end to it. If you study history with the aim of assigning blame, it's hard to find the beginning of what went wrong. Where did the blame begin? You can trace it all the way back to the myth of the Garden of Eden and blame Eve for offering Adam that forbidden apple.

Blaming others is not only useless, it's counterproductive. You may not like what happened but instead of blaming someone, bless them. Know that we are more than our actions and that blame only makes the situation worse.

When you think bad thoughts toward a politician, you are adding to their negativity. Better to say, "Why, bless their soul!" When I read in the news that a foreign military general was assassinated, instead of trying to figure out if he a was a good guy or bad guy, and should we have done that or not, I said, "Well, God bless that man." That made me feel better and brought some goodness to the situation.

We can do that every day. Most of the time when someone is angry at you, it is something that is triggered within themselves. Maybe they didn't realize what they did. Instead of reacting, try to understand their suffering that gave rise to their anger—and feel compassion. Think to yourself, "Well, bless that person. God bless their soul."

Yesterday I met a friend at the post office and he told me something bad about a mutual friend. I was tempted to not trust that mutual friend again. Then my friend told me something good about our acquaintance. This created ambiguity in my mind and I wondered if that mutual friend was good or bad.

I quickly resolved that dilemma by realizing that no matter what he had done, he had basic goodness. I said mentally, "God bless him," and decided to hold an image of him as a good man, that he had the light of God in his heart. For all I know, there may be people who say I did something bad, so I gave him the same grace I would want given to me. It comes back to what Jesus said:

Judge not, that you be not judged.

It's a great feeling when you can do that. Think of someone that hurt you and say, "Well, bless their soul." It's a relief you can feel. If you do something less than perfect, recognize your basic goodness and bless yourself. You can say:

God bless my soul.

The Buddhists philosophy is that we all have basic goodness, which means that the same light of awareness, the same love, is in all of us. Jesus said the same thing, "The Kingdom of Heaven is within you." You can say:

I Am good and everyone I see is good.
I love everyone and everyone loves me.

Think of someone that hurt you and instead of reacting, think:

Well bless their soul.

It's a relief, isn't it?

Importance of Self-Worth

We get some of these ideas about our lack of self-worth in childhood. There's the story about two dogs that met on the sidewalk and one dog said to the other, "What's your name?" He said, "Fido. What's yours?" The other dog replied, "My name is Bad Dog."

That's what his owners had said to him when he jumped on the sofa or tried to eat off the dining room table; they said, "Bad dog! Bad dog!" Well, the dog got the idea that was his name. Can you relate to that? We are all like that, too. When you were a child, your parents might have said "bad boy" or "bad girl" and that blame is still internalized within you. That blame, self-doubt, and lack of self-love needs to be healed. Meditate on your basic goodness and once again feel love for yourself.

If you go into a café, you might think, "These people are judging me, maybe they heard a negative story about me or they don't like my looks." You can change that anticipation of rejection by tuning in to your basic goodness. See the infant that you once were—now held within your heart. Say to that infant:

I love you (your name).

Holding that love in your heart, expand it and share your love with others by saying and feeling:

I know these people love me because "I Am Love." I know the love in their heart feels the love in my heart.

Close your eyes, then say and feel:

I Am good. I Am Love.

Feel the warmth in your heart and picture a golden sun with a pink light around it. Say and feel:

My love and goodness are radiating out to everyone around me, to everyone in this room, town, state, country, and world.

Realize that you are a good person. Say to yourself and feel:

I Am a good person and I Am loved.

Repeat with deep feeling and knowing:

I Am loved...I Am loved...I Am loved,

for I am Love.

If nobody has told you recently that they love you, know that everyone in our group loves you. I love you. Saint Germain loves you. Jesus loves you. And Violet Tara loves you. Most importantly, your God Presence that sustains you at every second loves you. Say and feel deeply:

I Am the embodiment of Divine love, radiating out to bless everyone I meet.

After a while you will notice how people react to you differently. You will feel more accepted, recognized, and loved for who you are.

Chapter 10

Violet Tara Meditation: Concise Form

This is the essence of the Violet Tara practice, given here in a concise form:

I call on Violet Tara to come forth. Saint Germain, please empower this practice. Manifest Violet Tara as the Goddess of Forgiveness in my life. Make Her a vibrant force for goodness, enlightenment, and freedom.

Violet Tara emerges from a beautiful violet mist before you. Her heart emanates pink light. In the center of Her heart is a golden sun. Say and feel:

Beloved Tara, please come forth in my life and world and be with me this week. I ask for Your blessings. Come forth and dissolve and consume anything less than perfection. Become one with me.

She comes toward you and dissolves into a ball of Violet Light, which enters your heart. You think and feel, "I Am Violet Tara." Feel the Violet Light enter every cell of your body, raising your frequency, dissolving all negative thoughts, feelings, judgements, and ill health. Say and feel:

*I Am Tara of Violet Fire,
I Am the Purity God Desires.*

Rise above the Earth in your new form as Violet Tara. Raise your hands and send a beam of Violet

Light out of each palm and out of your heart. You join together with others to form a circle around the Earth, sending Violet Fire down to the Earth wherever needed. Say and feel:

I Am Violet Tara, sending Violet Fire to Earth, into each and every situation that needs it, dissolving and consuming everything less than perfection, and raising all into its perfection.

Gradually, the Earth takes on a violet aura. Violet Light is spreading through our Solar System, Universe, and all Universes, raising everything into its perfect state. Say and feel:

I Am a being of Violet Fire, blazing forth wherever needed.

Gradually come back to Earth, still feeling yourself as Violet Tara, your body like an amethyst. If there had been any pain or stress in your body, it is now gone. Feel the Light and perfection in every cell. Say and feel:

I Am the Presence of Violet Tara,
I Am the purity God desires.
I Am the Violet Fire purifying my mind, body, and world.

Gradually bring that energy to your heart and feel the great God Flame that's anchored in the center of your chest as the Presence of God within you.

You are never for a moment separated from God. You have always been and will always be a God Presence. Even though you participate in this illusion of the limited physical form, you are eternal. Say, feel, and know:

I Am, I Am, I Know That I Am the Presence of God in action, right here and now, fully sustained throughout the coming week. I Am, I Am, I know that I Am the God in action in every situation. I Am Violet Tara, dissolving and consuming all obstacles. Reside above me and bless all I encounter.

Remember, when you see someone or something that appears less than perfect say:

Bless your soul.

Or:

God bless that.

Conclude with:

Thank you, Violet Tara. Thank you, Saint Germain. Thank you, beloved God Presence that I Am. I know you are with me always and that I Am You and You are me. We are a team, gaining love, wisdom, compassion, and Mastery in this world of illusion.

Chapter 11

I AM Affirmations

Great Divine Director:

I Am the Great Divine Director of my day.
I Am the Great Divine Director of my life,
my being, and my world.

I Am the Great Divine Director of all the
governments of the earth.

I Am the Great Divine Director of
my business.

I Am the Great Divine Director
of all my relationships.

I Am, come forth in and through me
throughout this day, bringing about the
Divine plan in all activity.

I Am being shown how to be a better person,
what qualities to develop,
and I Am that new person!

I call on the Ascended Masters to come forth
and help me in all I do. .

*I Am grateful to Saint Germain for making these teachings available to humanity.
I thank you and it is done.*

Violet Tara:

I Am Violet Tara.

*I Am Tara of Violet Fire,
I Am the Purity God Desires.*

I Am the Presence of God manifesting as Violet Tara, radiating purity, forgiveness, and freedom to humanity.

I Am Violet Tara, radiant Goddess from the heart of creation.

I Am Violet Tara dissolving and consuming all negativity in (location you choose).

I Am Tara of Violet Fire blazing the Violet Consuming Flame up, in, around, and through (location you choose).

Beloved Violet Tara, please reside above me in a beautiful pink lotus blossom. During the coming week, I ask You to come forth wherever needed and bless everyone I contact or even think about.

I Am Violet Tara, radiant Goddess from the Heart of Creation. I Am pouring forth love, purity, wisdom and forgiveness wherever needed, transmuting everything into its inherent perfection, and bringing God's Divine Plan to Earth this very moment. So be it.

I Am Violet Tara, blazing the Violet Consuming Flame throughout the Earth, dissolving and consuming everything less than perfection.

I Am Violet Tara healing my body this very instant.

I Am the Presence of Violet Tara. I Am the purity God desires.

I Am Violet Tara, dissolving and consuming all obstacles.

I Am in the center of the Earth, radiating Violet Fire outward through this planet and into space.

I Am Presence:

I Am the Presence of God that I Am.

I Am the Presence of the Living God.

I Am God in action throughout this day.

*I Am being shown the next step and
I am taking that step in perfect confidence.*

*I no longer see myself as a victim
For I Am God in action.*

*I Am, I Am, I Know that I Am the Presence
of God in action, right here and now, fully
sustained throughout the coming week.*

*I Am Divine Wisdom, Forgiveness, and Love
flowing forth to humanity.*

*I Am a White Fire Being from the heart
of the Great Central Sun.*

Love, Forgiveness, Abundance:

I Am forgiveness.

I Am a good person and loved by all.

*I Am loved...I Am loved...I Am loved,
for I am Love.*

*I Am the embodiment of Divine Love,
radiating out to bless everyone I meet.*

*I Am the abundance of God made manifest
in my hands and use so I can be
of benefit to humanity.*

Chapter 12

Extra Meditations and Practices

I Am a White Fire Being

Because this is a time when we need to strengthen the light within ourselves and on the entire planet, use the affirmation that calls forth your oneness with the God Presence as the Source of creation:

I Am the Presence of the Living God, for I Am a white fire being from the heart of the Great Central Sun.

The Central Sun is the etheric center of all the worlds and their universes, so you can think of it as the Godhead. It's where we all originated, so you're claiming your Godhood as a Divine Being from the center of creation. You can say that anytime, especially if you feel under pressure.

Everyone's I Am Presence is a ray from the Great Central Sun, but it manifests still as an individual ray and at the end of that ray is a ball of light. That is you and that will always be you. That I Am Presence is eternal; it exists outside of time and space. This is why we go within and affirm and amplify the light of our God Presence. We are calling it forth where we are just as we call forth the Violet Consuming Flame. You are a powerful being for you are the Presence of God. Wherever you are at this moment, you can change the course of the world.

Dialogue with your I Am Presence

In meditation with your I Am Presence you can, right this very moment, ascend into you God Self, this ball of golden light above you surrounded by a rainbow. The light and the energy in you increase and any negative energies are removed in the Violet Flame. Now you behold your I Am Presence and you say, "I Am That I Am That I Am."

Your I Am Presence conveys to you great happiness and replies, "At last you have found me. I want you to know I am here for you all the time at every moment. Just turn your attention to me. Contact me in your heart because that is where I reside in your physical body. I come forth also through your mind and through all your chakras but contact me through your heart. Not only am I there for you all the time, I Am you. Your so-called human self is just an extension of me, a puppet in the world of duality. The more you meditate on me, the more you become me, and become a fully conscious master in the world, capable of working miracles and of awakening everyone else to their true nature by the power of God that I Am."

Pour love and gratitude to your I Am Presence. Gradually, you become aware of your physical body below you and you bring that light of your I Am Presence down into your physical form. Feel it tingling with that Light and God consciousness in every cell down to your toes. When you bring that I Am Presence down into the physical body, the physical body begins to ascend. This is what they call in Tibet "attaining the Rainbow Body." So, ascension is achieved actually by descension. The I Am

Presence descends into the physical form and dissolves the illusory body. We think the physical body is the real body but actually that is the illusory body. When the I Am Presence dissolves that illusion, you are an ascended being and one with your God Presence.

Violet Tara Practice for the Earth

Stand either outdoors or in the middle of a safe place where you won't bump into anything. Remember, Tantra has three components: mantra (affirmation), mudra (movement or gesture), and visualization. Transform yourself into Violet Tara. You are immensely tall and powerful with a body like an amethyst. Your violet light radiates into space from your heart and hands. Stand in the sky above the North Pole (in Southern Hemisphere above the South Pole). Hold out your arms, palms downward in blessings. Turn clockwise, sending rays of violet light into the Earth, surrounding and illuminating it with your loving energy and violet light. Continue slowly turning clockwise three full revolutions. If you see any places that need specific attention, send rays of violet light down into them. While you are turning, keep repeating:

I am Tara of Violet Fire,
I am the purity God desires!

After you finish three revolutions, thank Violet Tara for manifesting through you:

Thank you, Violet Tara, for being One
with me to help the people of Earth.

Saint Germain Invocation

Beloved Master Saint Germain, please empower Violet Tara in my life right now, fully self-sustained, a living Goddess for the benefit of all. Oh, great Violet Tara, Beloved Divine Mother, You, who are an emanation of the Light from the Heart of Creation with which I Am One, I implore you. Release your Violet Fire of purification through my mind, feelings, and world. Purify and transmute wherever is needed this very moment. Thank You! I know it is already done.

Dedication of Merit

The Dedication of Merit is a classic Tibetan Buddhist prayer that's perfect as a prelude or conclusion to meditation. Merit, in Buddhist terminology, is not an award, but an energy you acquire through spiritual practice.

Throughout my many lives until this very moment; whatever virtue I have accomplished including the merit generated by this practice and all that I will ever attain, this I offer for the welfare of sentient beings. May sickness, war, famine, and suffering be decreased for every being while their wisdom and compassion increase in this and every

future lifetime. May I clearly perceive all experiences to be as insubstantial as the dream fabric of the night and instantly awaken to perceive the pure wisdom display in the arising of every phenomenon. May I quickly obtain enlightenment in order to work ceaselessly for the liberation of all sentient beings.
So be it.

An Invocation of Violet Tara

Beloved Goddess Tara, Mother of the Violet Flame of Forgiveness, help us overcome the illusions of the world. Free us from ignorance and help us achieve enlightenment. Grant us the ability to forgive and feel compassion for others. Clear all negative energy and raise our consciousness. We pray to you: Come to us now Violet Tara, Mother of the Violet Fire.

Meditation for Guidance

You may not hear this guidance audibly. You may simply wake up in the morning with a knowing. You may feel an impetus to do something different, or simply to complete projects you are working on. It doesn't mean there is going to be a dramatic change, but frequently big changes in our life do come unexpectedly. It's not that everything changes at once; you may be shown a plan that will unfold over time. As things come up in your life, you will have a knowingness that it is right. You will feel in your heart that this guidance is part of the Divine Plan. This is how meditation in action will manifest in your life.

Invoke your I AM Presence with the affirmation: In the morning when I awaken, I Am remembering what I have been shown and I Am manifesting God's Divine Plan in my life."

When you awaken, you may say and feel:

I now joyously accept the God Presence that I Am, and I rejoice in the Divine Plan my God Presence has for me. I Am the God Presence in action, now and always.

Inner Healing Using Mindfulness

I have spent so many years doing mindfulness practice that I erroneously assumed everyone knew how to do it and was using it to clear past trauma, stress, and dissolve ignorance. There is tremendous benefit in this method, which is part of Buddha's Eightfold Path to Self-Mastery.

Mindfulness is the combination of the solar and lunar paths. The moon represents the emotions and the hidden triggers linked to past traumas. As these come to the surface through mindful self-observation, they need to be examined in the light of the sun, the conscious mind, before whose rays they are dispelled.

The sun is one's innate goodness, the unfed flame that is one's true identity. That is why meditation on the sun within, using the outer sun as a reminder, is one of the most ancient spiritual paths. As one increasingly identifies with the sun, the darkness of ignorance and trauma is dissolved. Ideally, one incorporates both the sun and moon on the path of self-purification and enlightenment.

As an example, imagine you sit outside on a summer morning drinking your tea, when you notice an unpleasant smell. Over the course of a few days the smell becomes stronger and more offensive. Finally, you decide to hunt down the source of unpleasantness, and discover that it is coming from underneath a long ignored rock at the edge of the porch. You turn the rock over and discover mold growing there. Rather than throw the rock away or scrub it down, you simply leave the rock lying upside down in the sun. In a few days the smell is gone and your return the rock to its former position. In the same way, we may need to examine rocky places within our own psyches that need to be examined and exposed to the light of awareness. We don't need to dwell on those repressed issues obsessively but to allow them to dissolve in the light of our own basic goodness. What your attention is upon, you become; so put your attention on the inner sun.

In previous meditation instruction, I gave the method of observing the breath. To still your mind, feel the inbreath and outbreath, the rise and fall of your chest. When a thought arises, label it "thinking" and return to the breath. This is known as *shinay*, which means abiding in calmness. However, this is only the beginning of the complete practice.

What are these ideas and also emotions that arise and what do you do with them? Far from being the enemy, these apparent distractions are actually the doorway to the fire of self-purification and ultimate release from stress. The long-standing use of this practice is why Buddhist monks emanate peace and tranquility. It is also how the Tibetans, who were tortured and enslaved in camps by the communists, managed to not only survive but eliminate post-traumatic stress after their escape.

As you sit, observing your breath, ask yourself what you are feeling and from where the feelings arise. You may say, "I am feeling...,"and see what arises. Try to reduce the complex emotion that may be embedded in a movie of a past incident that may be stored in your mind to as few words as possible, maybe even one word, such as "fear" or "resentment."

Then you may say:

I am being shown the origin of this emotion.

All the while, however, you are continuing to observe your breath. This disengages the rational mind that wants to stay in control and keep you in the victim mode. The mindfulness established through observation of the breath allows you to see the workings of the human mind from a place of safety. From outside, you are able to observe how the ego functions, how it has enslaved you in delusion. You now observe it as you would a computer program you are trying to master. Getting angry or being impatient does not help.

Allow the various images to come to the surface of consciousness, but instead of reacting, you watch them from a distance as you would a movie on a screen in a theater. It is happening outside yourself and does not trigger the same response as when the incident happened.

What keeps you from being drawn back into the drama is not only your mindfulness but the awareness of your basic goodness. You are centered in your heart, what Trungpa Rinpoche called "the soft spot," where the Source of your Being is anchored. This Unfed Flame is the focal point of the Higher Self that gives you life, that beats your heart. Without Its Presence you would not live for a second. In feeling your Source, you become aware that you are loved by your God Presence. It not only beats your heart, makes your lungs breathe, It performs a thousand other functions to keep you alive and conscious. Feel gratitude to that Presence and expand that gratitude out as love, not only of self, but love for everyone and all life.

Now that you feel the love of your basic goodness, you can observe these images of past events, especially past stress, without being triggered. First of all, since the event happened in the past, there is no need to respond, no fight or flight necessary—only observation.

Keep coming back to the soothing rhythm of the breath, which is the Divine Mother sustaining you, the same Mother which birthed you and has always been with you, taking care of you.

As an image comes up, bless it, and bless the person associated with the event. Try to see that they too have a light in their heart, they have basic goodness, and are a child of the same Mother. See that their actions, even if intentional, arose out of ignorance. If they had truly understood the situation, especially of the long term implications of their actions, had known the karma they were creating, they would have behaved differently. This understanding that all harmful actions arise out of ignorance, is like a "Get out of jail free" card. Suddenly, the blame is gone. For example, you tell a child not to eat too many cookies but while you are gone, they eat the whole box. You were saving these cookies to serve to friends at your dinner party. You are also disappointed that your child has disobeyed. However, as you see the stomach pains and nausea of your child, the anger gives way to compassion. You remember that when you were a child you did the same thing. You also know this is a valuable lesson and part of your child's process of Self-Mastery. You don't need to punish them. The punishment is built in. So too is the punishment built into every disharmonious and hurtful act. You don't need to mete out the punishment. As you observe how this person hurt you in the past, you realize that the karmic retribution they have or will receive is inevitable and part of their growth and process of Self-Mastery. Their actions are also part of your growth and Self-Mastery. In fact, their hurtful action may be your own karmic retribution for something you did to them in a past life. Breathe in their pain, which you see as a dark karmic cloud around them, and exhale rays of light from your heart to theirs, dissolving the clouds and filling them with joy. Breathe in, breathe out, and let it go. Now you are both free.

You may say to yourself:

I am being shown why I created this incident in my life and what I can learn from it.

Then, you may see images of how you knew that person in a past life, how you injured them, and that this whole painful drama is the unfolding of a great lesson for both of you. It was something you both agreed to experience over a period of lifetimes to gain greater self-understanding and compassion. You were both Divine Beings at one time prior to descent into duality, and this involvement with them is for a higher purpose. The pleasure and pain, the ignorance and ultimate wisdom are part of the duality that enriches our being. Appreciate the richness of this world and the lessons you can learn here, knowing that ultimately the delusions and suffering dissolve into enlightenment and eternal freedom.

As you observe this person, you see they are also a child of God, and you say to them, "I bless you and release you into the arms of your own I Am Presence. I let go of all blame, stress, and feelings of guilt that no longer serve either of us, and release us both now into the eternal purity of our being. You can end by saying and feeling:

I Am, I Am, I know that I Am the Presence of the Living God that I Am. I go forth now, wholly Pure and Perfect, as a Master Presence under the guidance and protection of the Ascended Masters, on the path of Goodness and the Life Everlasting. So be it!

Most Concise Violet Tara Practice

Turn your attention inward and enter a state of non-dual awareness.

Visualize Violet Tara before you, myriad violet light rays streaming from Her heart and the palms of Her outstretched hands.

Request Saint Germain to empower your visualization and practice.

Invocation to Violet Tara:

Beloved Goddess, release your Violet Fire of Purification through me and dissolve anything less than perfection.

Merge with and become Violet Tara. Meditate on and repeat inwardly:

I AM Violet Tara.

Repeat Her mantra while feeling your oneness with Violet Tara:

I Am Tara of Violet Fire
I Am the Purity God desires.

Transmit Her blessings:

I Am Violet Tara pouring forth my blessings wherever needed. So be it!

Dissolve your visualization and return to wakeful awareness.

Ask Violet Tara to reside above you, seated on a moon and sun disk in a pink lotus blossom, and ask Her to go before you this day, blessing all.

Express your gratitude to Violet Tara. Repeat out loud the Sanskrit mantra of all 21 Taras (optional):

Om Tare Tuttare Ture Swaha (x3)

Chapter 13

Experiences with Violet Tara

These are actual experiences from people using Violet Tara in their lives. Some stories reference the Violet Tara Facebook group that includes people from around the world who are a wonderful community of practitioners.

Some mornings I am awakened by a wave of Violet Fire, which I know is coming from those of you doing the Violet Tara practice in various parts of the world. I do not often login to Facebook early in the morning, as I don't want to interrupt the energy; however, you can be sure I am doing the practice with you!
                                              -Peter Mt. Shasta

Today I was busy with family and preparations but enjoyed repeating Violet Tara affirmations and sent violet fire throughout the earth to all humanity, into all dimensions, time and space. It was beautiful. It is so incredibly supportive to know I am a part of a Violet Tara love team!
                                              -T.B.T., Iceland

The Violet Tara appeared to me today during meditation. I suddenly felt great sadness for no reason but proceeded to invoke and decree for Her assistance to clear my mental, emotional, physical and spiritual system of all negative energies. Shortly after, it seemed like a dark cloud had lifted! I felt great for the rest of the day.

-R.L., California

All I can think of to say is, oh my God!!! It was FANTASTIC!!! I don't know about the rest of you, my dearest Sangha, but there was something was very, very special about what took place this morning. It moved me to the very depths of my soul. Peter was so radiant, and when he shared with us his beautiful experience with Violet Tara...I don't think I've ever known of anyone who can convey the kind of blessings that come to us through him. The Radiation in our Blessed Group and POWER that is being given to us through the application and knowledge of the Great Violet Tara is unprecedented. Of this I am certain. I'm sorry if I sound like a fanatic but I am just over the moon! Thank you so much, my beloved Sangha, and thank you, Peter.

-Z.V., California

I used this today on the road here on Bali. Today, using the Violet Tara mantra, it stayed with me throughout the ride (a good two hours). Never happened before, so certainly a great start. The Violet Tara mantra came to stay strongly. I love it!

-S.A., Bali

Hi dear ones...I must have felt your energy because I suddenly thought of Violet Tara and did as Peter suggested, invoked Her silently and sent forth Violet Fire throughout the earth. When I came to the car and saw the clock, it was right at the time when you were meditating. How lovely to be so connected in beauty, blessings and love! I am starting the meditation now and looking forward to our Saturday wave of Violet Fire tomorrow!

-T.B.T., Iceland

I woke up in the night due to a headache but invoked Violet Tara's help to dissipate it. Shortly after, my headache went away and I fell back asleep. In another circumstance, I was confronted by two negative individuals. Negative emotions began to arise. I invoked the assistance of Violet Tara to dissolve the anger and negativity. My emotions began to stabilize and I weathered the toxic people without incident. My wife was very impressed that I didn't react to the situation.

-R.L, California

I had an errand in a mall and this time it was totally different than ever before. As I was walking the halls, I was inwardly blessing everyone with the Violet Fire and I felt the energy run through and around me. I felt totally sheltered from any disturbing energies. I finished my errand and walked out, feeling no drainage or fatigue, which is new for me. What a wonderful change.

-T.B.T., Iceland

I recently hit a frightening low point but had an amazing turnaround after we started the group meditations.

-R.O., Trinidad & Tobago

Maybe it was you (Peter) who ignited the flame for me. It came on all of a sudden. Thank you! When it happened, I logged in and saw the meditation for the

day had just started. How wonderful that we are all so connected and fueled by Violet Tara practice!
　　　　　　　　　　　　　　　　　-A.K., USA

Peter has offered beautiful and powerful guided meditations in his Sunday webinars. I had been having a problem with pain down the back of my leg for about a week. I was particularly uncomfortable last night when I recalled Peter's story about invoking the Violet Tara for help with tooth pain so I decided to do Violet Tara practice.

I followed the recording of the practice from the Sunday Webinar #3 in which Peter guided us to invoke Violet Fire for capitals and different cities. I paused the recording and envisioned Violet Light healing my hip and leg. As Violet Tara, I envisioned healing all people suffering with similar problems, Violet Light going into their bodies. While holding this, I repeated Violet Tara's mantra: "I Am Tara of Violet fire. I Am the purity God desires."

I continued listening to the recording and slept through the night without pain. I woke up feeling very relaxed in my right hip. I feel that this practice is very powerful. It is helping me experience my I Am Presence more fully.
　　　　　　　　　　　　　　　　-A.R., Colorado

I am so grateful for your teachings from Saint Germain and how they have impacted my life for the good. I wanted to share with you my recent experiences since I've started to do the Violet Tara practices from your book and webinars.

I have been seeking physical healing of various pains and chronic illness for many years now through many different modalities (diets, workshops, healers, bodywork, etc.). However, it seems that nothing really got to the core of the issues.

After practicing the Violet Tara meditation and taking your weekly webinar, I've noticed a shift in my overall mental and emotional state. I'm sometimes overwhelmed with love and acceptance for all of humanity and anyone I encounter during my day. I know Violet Tara is working with me on many levels. I am now viewing past events through a different lens, one of love and forgiveness.

It has saddened me to hear from my kids that their dad is still angry with me after many years. I know this hurts them. However, I now had the courage to do the right thing despite my fears and asked Violet Tara to be with us (during a meeting with him).

I am amazed at how loving and accepting the exchange went between us. We haven't been that open and honest since we first met. I told him how much I am sorry for the way things ended and any hurtful things I did; and I asked for his forgiveness. I thanked him for being a good husband and father to our kids. Surprisingly, we talked for an hour and a half, and he couldn't have been more gracious and loving. We shared our hurts and questions in a kind and loving manner and gave each other big hugs.

I can't tell you what a relief I feel now, such a load off my back. I feel hopeful that things will improve between us and our relationship with the kids. When I told my daughter about the meeting last night, she cried uncontrollable tears of joy.

I believe this is the missing link in healing the physical ailments I'm still dealing with, and that they will clear more easily now.

I am so grateful to you, Peter, for sharing these teachings with the world. It has been instrumental in opening my heart further. I look forward to continuing with your webinars in the future.
-Webinar participant, USA

Miracle of Forgiveness from Violet Tara!

One week prior to the first Violet Tara webinar, a childhood memory came forth during meditation that was very upsetting. As a result, I was feeling much anger and I didn't want to forgive.

The first Violet Tara webinar with Peter was so beautiful and so powerful that, after the webinar, I remained in the Violet Tara energy all through the night and into the morning, meditating on Violet Tara and repeating: "I AM Violet Tara of Forgiveness."

I brought in the anger and all the experiences that I needed to forgive, as well as the need for self-forgiveness. I remained in the Violet Tara energy and continued to repeat: "I Am Violet Tara of Forgiveness."

In the morning, when I emerged from meditation, all of the anger and resentment against others and myself were totally gone, and all that I could feel was Love.

Now, I am feeling only Love.

Thank you, Peter and Violet Tara for this miraculous gift of Forgiveness and Love. Four months after my original miraculous experience of forgiveness with Violet Tara, which transformed all anger and resentment against others and myself into Love, I am now having a new profound experience.

Having carried a lifetime core belief of "not being lovable," I am now miraculously actually feeling being Loved.

I have always been kind and loving. I have always felt love for others and for God but, prior to now, I was not able to receive love. I was not able to experience the love coming to me.

Now, I am feeling Loved—by God, by the Masters, by the Angels, by my Children, by my Grandchild, by my Friends, by the very air that I breathe.

For many years on my Spiritual Path I have known that God Is Love, and that we are God's Love— but I am now actually engaged in receiving this miraculous flow of Love coming to me and through me. I am eternally Grateful.

-J.D., California

The great Violet Tara is the Mother aspect of Creation as expressed through the activity of the Violet Consuming Flame....Accepting Her as my mother has stirred up some powerful feelings. These feelings haven't been all that pleasant, but I realize that this is a necessary part of my purification. I am learning to be the observer rather than the actor caught up in the drama.

My mother and I used to fight fiercely but I have learned not to react to her occasionally foul temperament.

Now, I find that I am becoming insulated from her anger by the Presence and compassion of Great Violet Tara. I feel loved and, probably for the first time in my life, I feel nurtured. I have finally begun to glimpse Peace.

Thank you, beloved Saint Germain and beloved Peter Mt. Shasta for bringing this aspect of the Divine Mother into our lives.
  -Z.V., California

Yesterday, I was feeling I caught a bad cold from our office. My head and my body seemed overheated. I worried that it might be more than a cold and felt down. I made the call by closing my eyes and visualizing Violet Tara in front of me. I asked my I Am Presence to blaze the Violet Flame through me and after multiple inner I Am affirmations I felt the magic of the Violet Light blaze through and purify my body, mind and feelings. Now I am back to normal and feel amazing.
  -S.S., Toronto

Printed in Great Britain
by Amazon